SELF-PUBLISH YOUR BOOK LIKE A PRO

AN ENTREPRENEUR'S GUIDE TO BECOMING A PUBLISHED AUTHOR

BECKY WARRAK

RAVEN
CREST
BOOKS
PUBLISHING

Copyright © 2024 Becky Warrak

All rights reserved.

The right of Becky Warrak to be identified as the author of this work has been asserted by her in accordance with the Copyright, Designs and Patents Act 1988

No part of this publication may be reproduced, stored in a retrieval system or transmitted in any form or by any means including photocopying, electronic, recording or otherwise, without the prior written permission of the rights holder, application for which must be made through the publisher.

First Edition 2024

ISBN: 978-1-7392592-6-6

Cover design by Miblart
Published by Raven Crest Books

Author's Note

As the owner of family-run publishing company Raven Crest Books, I am over the moon to present this self-publishing guide for entrepreneurs.

Writing can be a daunting and lonely place, and self-publishing even more so, which is why I wrote this book—to guide entrepreneurs through their self-publishing journeys as painlessly as possible, whilst feeling like they have a team of support behind them, cheering them all the way to the finish line.

Raven Crest Books' own journey as a publishing services company began back in 2011, not long after the launch of the Amazon Kindle and KDP.

Fast forward to 2024, and the world of self-publishing has become more accessible than ever—the industry is flying. However, with accessibility comes a rise in quantity and a drop in quality of book production. While self-publishing is a fabulous book-creating journey on which to embark, it's important to do it properly so the book industry at large is not destroyed by the decline in the quality of books being published. It is also necessary to uphold high standards to ensure that becoming a published author remains credible.

As an experienced entrepreneur myself, I know how hard it can be to stand out in a saturated marketplace. This is why I am passionate about helping entrepreneurs like you gain the credibility that you deserve to grow *your* business.

I created this guide to give online coaches the tools they need to be able to turn their knowledge into a published book. And to ensure that if you are going to take the self-publishing route, you are fully equipped for the journey, the investment, and the challenge.

Raven Crest Books is a small boutique company, and we are picky about the books we publish as a publishing imprint. However, of the books we have in our catalogue, we have sold over 219,000 books worldwide.

Our recent rebrand into the world of non-fiction publishing for online coaches means we can now focus our attention on advocating strongly for online coaches and bringing those coaches into the limelight by publishing their books—coaches whose job it is to guide, coach, and help others achieve their goals.

And what better way to boost your business into the space it needs to be in than to publish your own work and become a credible author in your industry?

Maybe you are writing a self-help book to extend the platforms your clients can access your advice from, or a step-by-step guide to walk your readers through a specific process within your business's niche. Or maybe you're writing about a significant journey in your life in memoir or autobiographical format that may provide relatability and help your audience decide they want to work with you.

Whatever business-related outcome you want to achieve from publishing your book, you will be able to achieve it with the help of this book.

This book alone holds enough information to ensure you can self-publish your work to a high standard. If you feel you may also need visuals, video tutorials, or simply require support, guidance, and accountability on your self-publishing venture then check out *The Self-Publishing Membership* to upgrade your self-publishing experience. Scan the QR code below for more information.

By the end of this book, you will know exactly how to self-publish your manuscript *and* market it to your ideal readership. Because let's face it, you could write the best book in the world, but if you don't market it, you're as good as hiding your book under a rock. Marketing is a non-negotiable if you want your book to sell and, unlike other self-publishing guides, this book goes into book-marketing strategies right from the word *go*.

So, without further ado, let's get started!

FAO: Members of the *Self-Publishing Membership*

If you're reading this book following a sign-up to our *Self-Publishing Membership,* welcome! It's great to have you on board. With the membership, you have bonus access to the video tutorials included in the membership. This vault of videos is ideal for people who think they may struggle with the more technical aspects of publishing.

Not only this, but you also have access to the owners of Raven Crest Books for support, twice monthly, throughout your self-publishing journey. Be sure to make use of these sessions and maximise your time with the owners and industry guest experts.

As a member, remember to join our exclusive Facebook group, 'The Self-Publishing Membership Support Group (by Raven Crest Books)' to check in with your peers and ask the admins any questions you might have during your self-publishing journey. Scan the QR code below to head to the group straightaway.

Good luck and enjoy the ride. We can't wait to see your finished products!

Contents

1) Is Self-Publishing Right for You?............................. 1
2) Self-Publishing Costs v. The Self-Publishing Mindset 9
3) Hiring a Freelancer...19
4) Marketing: The Early Stages...................................26
    1) Target Audience 30
    2) Author Branding and Website....................34
    3) Social Media 42
    4) Mailing Lists..49
    5) Beta-Readers 54
    6) ARC Team 56
    7) PR...61
    8) Podcasts 64
5) Create Your Publishing Timeline 66
6) Write a Sales-Converting Back Cover Blurb 72
7) Design an Eye-Catching Book Cover 76
    1) Demographic and Research 78
    2) Images, Stock Photos, and Licences 83
    3) Typography...88
    4) The Back Cover and Full Sleeve 91
    5) Sizing...94

- 6) Print Standards 97
- 7) Hiring a Designer and Buying Premade 100

8) The Re-Read and Edit 105
- 1) Re-Reading Your Manuscript 106
- 2) Beta-Readers/Manuscript Review 108
- 3) Hiring an Editor 114
- 4) Different Types of Editors 117
- 5) Proofreading 123
- 6) Extra Copy 128
- 7) ISBNs 138

9) Transform Your Manuscript 141
- 1) Book Layout 144
- 2) Copyright page 146
- 3) Table of Contents 152
- 4) Fonts and Font Size 155
- 5) Page Sizing, Margins, and Alignment 158
- 6) Headers and Footers 162
- 7) General Structure 165

10) Print On Demand (POD): Platform Overview 169
- 1) KDP 172
- 2) Lightning Source 177
- 3) Ingram Spark 182

11) KDP Account Set-Up 185
- 1) Set-Up 186

- 2) Description, Categories, and Keywords 188
- 3) Content 195
- 4) Proof Copies 197
- 5) Pre-Order 200
- 6) Hit Publish 206
- 7) A+ Content 209
- 8) Printing and Author Copies 212
- 9) Amazon Author Page 216
- 10) KDP Select 218
- 11) Pricing and Royalties................................221
- 12) Reports..225

12) Marketing: The Launch and Beyond 226
- 1) The Press Release 227
- 2) Reviews, Social Media, and Mailing Lists ..234
- 3) Giveaways and Collaborations 239
- 4) Book Signings and Launch Events.............241

13) A Final Note...247

14) Contact Details 251

15) References..252

Glossary of Terms

ARC – Advanced Reader Copy

A completed and formatted version of your manuscript that is sent out for feedback, PR, and marketing purposes prior to publication

ASIN – Amazon Standard Identification Number

An identification number given to products sold on Amazon to assist with product indexing

CMYK – Cyan, Magenta, Yellow, Key

Colours used in the printing process

GDPR – General Data Protection Regulation

A piece of European legislation that protects personal information, outlining several requirements businesses must follow to process that data legally *(Ref 23)*

High Resolution

Images with a higher concentration of pixels or dots, resulting in better quality and clarity of the image. Anything 300 PPI or DPI or over is usually considered to be high resolution *(Ref 24)*

ICA – Ideal Client Avatar

A technique used to identify and hone your target audience in order to produce specific marketing content

ISBN – International Standard Book Number

A unique number assigned to every published book

KDP – Kindle Direct Publishing

Amazon's own print-on-demand platform

MS – Manuscript

An original document written by the author before it goes through the publishing process to become a book

POD – Print On Demand

A method of creating a product individually as soon as the customer makes a purchase, rather than needing to hold and sell stock

ROI – Return On Investment

Money you make as a result of investing in something

SEO – Search Engine Optimisation

The process of improving your website to increase its visibility in Google, Microsoft Bing, and other search engines *(Ref 22)*

USP – Unique Selling Point

Key positive aspects of your business that you can draw upon to attract clients—aspects that differentiate you from your competitors.

Chapter 1
Is Self-Publishing Right for You?

If you're here, you have probably either finished your manuscript or are thinking of writing one and want to be fully prepared before you embark on your book writing and publishing journey. Whether having your book published is a personal milestone of yours, or an entrepreneurial mastermind move in your business's marketing strategy, choosing the right publishing method is important to ensure your book achieves what you want it to.

At this point, you may know nothing about publishing and are on a researching mission to discover your options before you decide which route to take. Generally speaking, there are three main options when it comes to getting your book published: traditional publishing, partnership publishing (also known as hybrid publishing), and self-publishing.

Many people see traditional publication as the holy grail of publishing and have their sights set on being offered a big shiny book deal. If you're an entrepreneur and have specific goals you want to achieve as a result of your book's publication, it's important to consider the alternative options. Even though being published traditionally is seen as a huge accolade, depending on what you want to achieve from publishing your book, there may be intricacies of the traditional process that make your overall business objectives harder to reach.

Let's break these publishing methods down:

Traditional Publishing

When you think about becoming published, you may automatically assume the traditional meaning of the word. This means that the manuscript will be picked up by a publishing house (such as *Penguin Random House* or *HarperCollins*, or even smaller more boutique publishing houses), the author receives a book deal and a medium-to-large sum of money, and then the publishers take care of the whole publishing process.

The main aspects that define this method of publishing are:

- No cost to the author
- An author payout
- Your book will be sold in physical bookshops nationwide (depending on the retail connections and the size of the publisher) as well as retailing online
- Lower author royalties

Traditional publishing houses will usually have their own print set-up with offshore printers which enables them to print in bulk at relatively low costs. Contrary to popular belief, traditional publishing houses do not always offer marketing and PR as part of their business model. Generally speaking, the big PR budgets are saved for celebrities and well-known authors. If you do enquire with traditional publishing houses, be sure to clarify how their book marketing process works and whether you'll be assigned PR and marketing resources as part of your contract.

Author payouts are a direct reflection of the predicted return on investment (ROI) the publisher expects your book to bring them. For example, if you're David Beckham the publisher can hazard a guess that the revenue they will generate from publishing his book is going to be pretty immense. Therefore, they would pay David proportionately from their projections. It's worth bearing in mind that traditional publishers usually only pay between 10 and 25% royalties. On the flip side, it's likely that the volume of books they sell will be probably be greater than if you were to opt for a different method of publishing.

These are a few of the main drawbacks of publishing traditionally that should be considered:
- No guarantee of getting signed
- Some publishing houses only accept submissions from authors with an agent
- No guarantee of finding an agent
- Lack of author involvement in the process
- Large amount of time taken between submission and publication

It can take authors years to get their manuscript accepted by a traditional publisher, quite simply because the publishers can afford to be picky and will only publish (and invest in) what they can guarantee will make them a high monetary return. There are also a huge number of manuscripts submitted daily by budding authors, so competition is extremely high. Not to mention the fact that many publishing houses don't accept submissions from an author if they don't have an agent – which means you could also waste years of your time querying agents too!

If you do go down the traditional publishing route and receive a book deal from a big publishing house, have a think about whether you're happy to sign over your manuscript and have little involvement with how it is produced. This will vary per publisher, and you are likely to get *some* input, but often the publisher will take your book on with a very distinct plan of how they will edit, design, and market your book to make them as much money as possible. Obviously different publishers have different values and principles, but if you have a precise vision of how you want your book to turn out, it's important to do your research and find a publisher who will incorporate your ideas into the project.

Partnership Publishing (Hybrid Publishing)

This type of publishing bridges the gap between self-publishing and traditional publishing. The 'partnership' aspect indicates that you work in partnership with the publishers to produce your book together. Partnership publishers do the same work that you would do by self-publishing, but they do it all for you. They have much more experience in the market, they have many more contacts and experts working for them, and they will produce your book to a high standard.

Partnership publishers are the middleman, and they effectively work as an agency to bring you all the services you require conveniently in one place. Some partnership publishers work as a one-man band and are skilled and qualified enough to do all the work themselves, whereas other hybrid publishers will have well-vetted and experienced freelancers working as part of their team.

You may also see these types of services labelled as 'self-publishing services', because that's technically what they are. On the whole, hybrid publishers and partnership publishers will complete the whole process for you, from editing to online upload (some hybrids have their own print set-up and distribution process too) whereas self-publishing service companies often offer individual services to aid self-publishing authors, as well as the full package.

Partnership publishers will also have their own publishing imprint so authors that go through a hybrid or partnership publisher will receive the accolade that their book has been produced by a publishing house. Their company logo will probably appear on the book's finished cover and/or spine.

Often hybrid or partnership publishing companies will have evolved from someone who has self-published their own books, become very good at the process and familiar with the industry, and then set up their own publishing company to help other people become published authors too.

Factors that define a hybrid publisher:
- It's a paid service (upfront costs to the author)
- The end product will predominantly be available to purchase online only
- Higher author royalty payouts than traditional publishers offer

If you decide to go through a partnership publisher, again, it's important to do thorough research to find the right company to work with. This includes scrutinising where your money is being spent and what book marketing is included in your package.

Self-Publishing

Self-publishing has become an extremely popular method of publishing among independent writers, authors, and business owners due to the simple fact that publishing your own book has become so attainable by the online technology available to us. Self-publishing is exactly what it says on the tin: the author will take full control of turning their completed manuscript into a published piece of work. This includes taking charge of all the following processes:

- Editing
- Proofreading

- Formatting
- Book cover design
- Online platform upload
- Book marketing

As a self-publishing author, you will project-manage the whole process, allocate your budget accordingly, decide where your own skills lie and where to outsource, and have complete control of how the finished product turns out.

There are many benefits to self-publishing:

- Receive 100% of the royalties
- Choose where your book retails
- Choose how to print your book
- Flexible deadlines to fit around your goals
- Handpick the professionals you outsource to
- Publish your book in months rather than years
- Own the publishing rights to your book
- Have complete creative freedom with the production of your manuscript

If reading about self-publishing has you fired up, you're in the right place! If you're an entrepreneur with aims of using your book as part of your overall business marketing strategy, self-publishing is the perfect option. Not only do you have complete control over how the finished product looks, but you're also able to create flexible deadlines and launch dates that suit your business schedule and marketing goals. You can tie your book launch in with other product or new service launches, set a pre-order to create excitement around your business, use your book as a lead magnet to encourage people to sign up to your latest online course—the world is your oyster!

These ideas will all be addressed in much more detail in the marketing chapters of this book. But first, you'll need an exceptional product to market. In the next chapter, we'll address the costs involved in self-publishing and also discuss the importance of going into this journey with the right mindset, so that 'exceptional' is something you can achieve.

Chapter 2
Self-Publishing Costs v. The Self-Publishing Mindset

Technically speaking, the act of self-publishing is free. Writing a manuscript is free. Uploading your manuscript to an online platform can also be free. Hell, even getting your book printed is free since the POD process has been established. But free doesn't always mean you'll achieve the best results possible, and it also doesn't always mean 'free'.

This is where cost meets mindset. If you're looking to self-publish your book without spending a penny, this probably isn't the book for you. This chapter will help you rethink the way you perceive self-publishing which, in turn, should help you work out how much money you are willing to spend on publishing your book.

It's OK if you weren't originally planning to spend any money on publishing your book. Keep an open mind and your book's best interests at heart, and let's see if you still aren't willing to invest by the end of this book.

Analogy time. Self-publishing for free is a bit like attempting to build your own wardrobe without spending a penny. You could technically build it using upcycled wood from your garage, or perhaps an old piece of furniture. You already have all the tools—hammer, saw, nails, paint—required to build it in your shed, lying in wait for their moment of glory, so in this instance, yes, building your own wardrobe is free. And of course, your labour is free too. But would it look great? Maybe. Would it stand the test of time? Who knows?

The point is, whilst the idea of building your own wardrobe is free, what that really means is that your labour is free. But is your labour *really* free? What is building that wardrobe taking you away from? Where could your time be spent more productively? An expert could build a bespoke wardrobe for you in maybe half a day, but how many days or weeks would it take you to learn how to do it and then execute the task?

And what about if you didn't already have the necessary tools you would need to build a wardrobe to a good standard? What if the quality of the wood in your garage is questionable, and the tools are going to set you back a fair wedge from the local hardware store?

The question you have to ask yourself is this: can I produce a product to the same standard that a professional company would be able to without spending a penny?

Even if you do decide that your labour is going to be the cheapest part *and* you have the time to do it, the very least you should do is invest in some good quality wood, buy the tools you need, and follow a few decent tutorials.

The same applies to your book.

If you don't invest in the materials and know-how to get your book published, the outcome will likely be substandard.

Money is often a sticky subject for many people, so let's jump straight in here. The very first step towards publishing your book is working out how much money you are comfortably willing to spend on doing so. Therefore, prepare to embrace: The Self-Publishing Mindset.

The Self-Publishing Mindset: Knowing Your Book Goals

In order to establish how much money you want to invest in self-publishing your book in order to grow your business, think for a moment about what your goals are for your manuscript. What do you want to *achieve* from publishing your book? Once you have identified what you want to get out of book-publishing, you'll be able to decide more confidently how much you are willing to put into it.

Here are some of the reasons you might want to write and publish a non-fiction book as an entrepreneur:

- Add another revenue stream (royalties)
- Lead generation/lead magnet
- Reach a wider network of people

- Raise your status and credibility in your field
- Present yourself as an expert in your industry
- Increase event speaker and guest expert opportunities
- Increase marketing and PR opportunities
- Increase website traffic and generate new opportunities for advertisement monetisation
- Coach-to-client relatability
- Increased mailing list sign-ups
- Stand out from the crowd in a saturated market

Do these sound like good reasons to publish a book?

The great thing about writing a book is that you could be at any stage of running your business for it to provide you with the above benefits. Let's break it down further by giving you some real business examples from people at different stages of their careers:

The Start-Up Entrepreneur

Mark is one to two years deep into his running his small business. He's passionate about it, he's making a small income per month but potentially not enough to quit his day job yet.

He knows he wants his business to go places, and he provides exceptional services to his clients, but he often feels like his business is hiding under a rock. He's not reaching his ideal customers, and he's just not stacking up against the bigger names in his industry. He doesn't have a great deal of time to dedicate to learning about social media marketing, which means his followers amount to hundreds rather than thousands. Mark feels like he's banging his head against a wall trying to drum up hype around his business and prove to the world that his services will change peoples' lives.

Mark's goal: Publish a book to use as part of his marketing strategy to gain credibility amongst his peers, gain social proof, and become more visible to more clients. End goal: reach and sign up more clients, increase business revenue, quit his day job, and turn his side hustle into his full-time career.

The Investment: Should equal any amount that he's willing to put into other forms of marketing.

If you are using a book to scale your business, or use as a 'business card' to reach more people, this is marketing. Marketing costs money because, generally, marketing is a sound way to reach a nice little ROI (Return On Investment). If you're planning on making money from your book, not necessarily from book sales but from the expansion of your business, you need to invest a decent amount to make the whole exercise worthwhile.

The Established Entrepreneur

Penny owns a thriving online life-coaching business, which has grown over the years, and she even employs someone to do her social media for her and a virtual assistant to handle her admin. Sales are good, Penny can get away with working just a few hours per day. But she often wonders how she can prove she is an established entrepreneur—an expert in her industry with a wealth of experience and clients behind her. She wants those expert speaker positions, but how can she stand out from the crowd on applications? What makes her so 'established' and trusted in her field? Does she have the Instagram or TikTok followers to back up her reputation? Because isn't that what measures credibility these days…?

Penny's Goal: Increase sales, prove her level of experience, and open the door to expert speaker opportunities.

The Investment: Much the same as the start-up entrepreneur, if you're expecting to see a monetary increase or achieve a life goal of becoming an advocate in your field from publishing your book, you need to invest to make sure the finished product is a credible piece of work. There's nothing credible about a book that's cut so many corners it looks like an origami swan.

The Small-Biz Owner with a Story to Tell

Bella created her mindset coaching business based on her own life experiences and the journey she went on to overcome the hurdles life threw at her. She's the business owner who's overcome all odds to achieve what she never thought she could achieve.

Now she's coaching others how to do the exact same thing.

She wins people over with her charming, warm nature and her willingness to bare all and be completely raw about her life and how she got to where she is today. Her problem is getting in front of the people who need her help in order to help them.

Bella's goal: Bella is writing her book to get her story out into the world, to leave her legacy, to make sure her grandchildren know what she went through, and to ensure that no one has to go through what she did. She wants to inspire, encourage, and coach others who have been on a similar journey.

The Investment: There's no point trying to leave a legacy if you aren't prepared to put some money behind the project. Bella's story is a testament to her and her character, and it deserves to be written and published properly in order to reflect the standards that she upholds within her business and her life—and that she wishes to uphold for the future clients she helps.

The point is that, generally speaking, a book is not worth publishing if it has not been invested in. If you've made the effort to write it, do yourself proud and reach the goals you want to achieve by putting your money where your mouth is.

So, get checking your bank accounts, pull some savings, put money aside, cut down on the £50 takeaways and maybe cancel your TV streaming subscription for a few months. Change your mindset from 'I can't afford to publish a book' to 'I need to invest in my book for it to achieve what I want it to achieve'.

Now that we've established that self-publishing to a high standard is not free, let's break down the necessary costs in the table that follows. This should give you an idea of the total amount you should start putting aside to achieve your book publishing goals:

	DELIVERABLES	LOW END COST	HIGH END COST
BETA-READER	Manuscript (MS) review and report	£50	£600+
EDITOR	**Developmental Editor** Overall content edit	£1,000	£2,500+
	Copyeditor Overall structural edit	£700	£2,000+
COVER DESIGNER	Personalised full cover sleeve to your specifications	£150	£700+
PROOFREADER	Full MS proofread to correct typos and grammatical errors	£200	£1,000
FORMATTER	Full typsetting to transform MS from a Word doc into book format	£80	£250+
ISBN	Individual ISBN	£100	
PROOF COPIES	1x proof copy	£4	£10
TOTAL	All work delivered and MS ready for POD publication	£2,284	£7,160

NOTE: *Not all manuscripts* need *more than one editor. Different types of editors are addressed in the chapter 'The Re-Read and Edit' on page 106.*

If you buy ISBNs in bulk, they cost less.

Whether you have enough budget to splash out at the top end of the spectrum, or enough money to see you through the cheaper end of self-publishing with established freelancers, you should now have a tangible figure in mind that you are happy to spend on publishing your book.

***NOTE:** By 'the cheaper end', this means as low-end as you can probably go without jeopardising the quality of your book. There are plenty of good professionals out there who charge not-so-extortionate prices. 'High-end' refers to hiring extremely experienced and sought-after freelancers who would be preferred by top-end authors with large budgets behind them.*

Chapter 3
Hiring a Freelancer

During the self-publishing process, you may hit a stumbling block and consider opting to hire some help.

Firstly, please do not feel like you have failed at self-publishing if you need to outsource! Self-publishing can sometimes be a labour of love, and often a long-winded task, and barely anyone will be qualified with the necessary skills to complete the self-publishing process completely alone. Maybe you will excel at cover design but struggle with some of the more technical aspects like POD platform management. Maybe you have a love-hate relationship with Word and can't get your head around the formatting (see page 141.

Being able to choose your own team of people who will contribute to the creation of your book is one of the beautiful things about self-publishing. In no other method of publishing would you be this involved with the experts helping to produce your book.

In self-publishing, the relationship between author and editor can often become a close one as you work together to reach perfection. In traditional publishing, you get less control; you may not be granted approval over the cover design or title of your book or you may not be allowed to make edits to the text after a certain point.

Take this power and use it wisely. If outsourcing, craft your team of specialists carefully and make sure you maximise each of their skills.

Whichever aspect you need assistance with, knowing when to ask for help is a skill in itself. You could be a jack of all trades, but some tasks call for a master. Hopefully, this brief chapter will help you find where these masters are hiding.

If you've decided to go down the route of hiring a freelancer (or a few freelancers) to do any of your publishing work for you then you'll need to know where to find the *right* ones.

These days it's easy enough to find someone to do pretty much anything for you online, but will they be any good at it? Or will they take your money and run...?

It's certainly tricky to differentiate the pros from the con artists. So here are a few places you can hope to find professionals who will deliver your money's worth:

- Reedsy
- Social Media (Facebook, Facebook groups, Instagram)
- LinkedIn

- 99 Designs (this is an auction-based design platform, and it's fun too!)

Trusted Facebook groups are a great place to find professional freelancers, and usually they will come recommended by other group members. *Trusted* is the emphasized word here; trust really is key—there are a ***lot*** of spammy Facebook groups out there with people posing as anyone they like, eager to take your money! Get to know the group, get to know the members, suss out who the 'Top Contributors' are and who you can trust to pass on accurate information.

Once you think you've found some good options to work with on any of the above platforms, next comes due diligence, which comes in the form of questions, research, and more questions.

As a company, we rarely take on new freelancers without them being referred to us through existing contacts. And when we do take on new freelancers, there's a process we follow to ensure we only hire the best. For example, our general process for hiring new editors is as follows:

- **Start with general questioning**

Ask them a string of initial questions about their relevant experience for the job.

- **Dig deeper into specific requirements**

Ensure they have the correct experience within our niche (for example, because we publish non-fiction, we wouldn't take on a fiction editor. But furthermore, we hunt around to find editors who also have experience within the exact niche of the book being edited. For example, if we are publishing a memoir, we'll look for an editor who specifically edits memoirs).

- **Ask for a sample edit**

Ask for a sample edit (2,000 words max) so you can see how they work, how they deliver their feedback, and what kind of edits they are likely to make to your manuscript. If you don't like some of the things they've done, but in general you like the way they work, be honest with the editor and let them know what you would have preferred. In turn, they should be honest with you and tell you whether your requests are within their remit, or whether you'd be better off seeking an alternative editor.

Some editors will provide a sample edit for free with the aim that they will secure a future payment with you. Others may charge a small fee, usually at their normal price per word rate.

- **Arrange an interview/Zoom call**

If all the other boxes have been ticked, arrange a face-to-face (or Zoom call) 'interview'. This is important to make sure the connection is there. As an author, you want to connect with your editor to make sure they are on the same wavelength as you. We specifically want to ensure they are listening to what we are saying. Listening is key if the editor is to know exactly how you want your book to turn out. Personality is also key. If your book is written in a light-hearted, jovial tone, you would want to hire someone who is on the same level as you—you want to make sure your voice remains strong throughout your manuscript and isn't edited out.

For us, knowing who our editors are means that, as a publisher, we are in a better position to pair our authors with the perfect editor for them.

As a self-publishing author, you can follow the same protocol that Raven Crest Books uses to ensure that you hire the best too—because your book deserves it!

We apply the same formula to other freelancers, too, including formatters, proofreaders, and cover designers.

Remember, you are completely within reason to create a contract and ask the freelancer to sign it if it makes you feel more comfortable about handing over money to a stranger. This way you can document the deliverables, timeframes, and fees. It's also a great way to make sure that you and the freelancer are singing from the same hymn-sheet and no details are left out. Alternatively, a lot of freelancers have their own contracts they will use for each new job.

You don't need to be a lawyer to put together a simple contract. You can use an online search engine to find a freelancer contract template or you can create your own from scratch. These are the kind of things you might want to include in a freelancer contract:

- Contract start and end date
- Parties involved—author and freelancer. (This might be their full name or their business's name.)
- Valid addresses for both parties
- Deliverables—the service they are providing to you. (Be as precise as you want. You could simply write 'Editing', or you could document the exact deliverables such as 'Line-by-line editing focusing on language and tone'.)
- Timings and deadlines
- Scenarios where you will not pay for their services or will pay a reduced rate. (E.g., if they don't complete the services within the agreed timeframes.)
- Signatures and signature dates

Pro-Tips for Avoiding Scams

We want you to hire the right freelancers, so here are some pointers to bear in mind when searching for the right professional, to prevent getting scammed:

- Ask for testimonials and examples of their previous work

- Ask for a sample edit
- Ask to see their website and social media profiles
- Look for a professional who specialises in the specific niche of your own manuscript
- Ask about payment plans to invest your money safely
- Get a contract in place to protect your money

And most importantly, remember, you get what you pay for. If someone is telling you they'll edit your book for a tenner, I'd run a mile! On the other hand, maybe they're a naturally talented, newly-graduated editor with minimal previous experience who's looking to build a portfolio before raising their prices.

Trust your gut, protect yourself, and ask as many questions as possible!

Chapter 4
Marketing: The Early Stages

1. Target Audience
2. Author Branding and Website
3. Social Media
4. Mailing List
5. Beta-Readers
6. ARC Team
7. PR
8. Podcasts

You might be thinking that this is a weird place for the marketing chapter to be—at the beginning of the book. Don't you market a book once its published? There's currently nothing to market!

Wrong.

There's you. We need to market YOU. The author. The business owner. The storyteller. The star of the show! It would actually be weirder if this section was at the end of the book because marketing is a mammoth task and it should *not* be an afterthought if you want your book to be successful.

You also need to start marketing the *idea* of your book. Because although a physical book doesn't exist yet, the idea does.

People tend to think that writing is the hard part of the whole publishing process, and that once they have their first draft complete, they can stick their manuscript on KDP, hit publish, and let the royalties roll in.

As you have probably sensed by now, there is more to it than that!

Your book is going to go sweet nowhere without putting in some hard graft on the marketing. Marketing is maybe the most time-consuming part of the publishing process. Not because the tasks are particularly difficult, but because of the volume of methods and tools you'll implement and follow through with to get your book seen.

These days, making your book live to the world is literally as simple as pressing a button. But getting people to buy your book is a whole different story. And it begins right at the beginning, even as early as whilst you are still writing your book.

The amount of effort you put into your book marketing relates back to your book goals and what you want to gain from your book's publication. The amount of success your book achieves for you—whether 'success' looks like further reach, more clients, or increased revenue—should directly reflect in your marketing efforts.

If you're not overly bothered about book sales or increased business revenue but want to have your book published for the sake of the 'published author' title and credibility, then marketing your book might be low on your to-do list. (But imagine how much more credible you would be if you had a *successful* published book.)

But if you want to reach 'best-selling author' status, have people raving about your book, and clients queuing up to work with you, roll up your sleeves and be prepared to put in some solid marketing hours.

Although the idea of marketing may scare you, try to embrace it and enjoy it. Marketing is an excuse for you to rave about your business, shout about your book, and tell the world how amazing you are! And the fact that you have written a book makes you ten times more interesting to your audience and gives you much more to talk about in your marketing campaigns.

In this chapter, you'll learn exactly what you need to do to market your book and create a following of people who want to read it. There may be parts of this section that you are already aware of and have implemented previously through the growth of your business (which you can also apply to marketing your book), so please feel free to skip past these sections.

You'll notice a second marketing section at the back of the book. It lives there because a lot of its content includes marketing techniques you can apply (and can sometimes *only* apply) after your book is published. But there are also marketing ideas in Chapter 12 that you might need to start implementing during the publishing process.

After you've finished this chapter, jump to Chapter 12 (page 226) and familiarise yourself with the other aspects of marketing so you can decide where it all fits in your publishing timeline (see 'Create Your Publishing Timeline' Chapter 5, page 66).

1) Target Audience

If you're an entrepreneur and you've owned your business for a few years, chances are you are fully aware of who your target audience is. It's very hard to create a successful business without knowing who your people are and where to find them.

Knowing and understanding your target audience is key for your business's marketing strategy, and it's no different when it comes to marketing your book.

When you're writing a non-fiction book, the whole point of your book is usually to provide value or solve peoples' problems. So, how do you know who that someone is if you haven't identified them yet?

Identifying your target audience early on will not only help you hone your audience and the target market that you will sell to, but it also helps refine the way you write your manuscript. Knowing your audience also allows you to write very specifically to the exact person you want to buy your book when its published.

Your manuscript should literally be aimed at your target audience, therefore the language and tone used throughout your book needs to be appropriate to your people to ensure your book is readable, relatable, and understandable.

A good way to work out who your target audience is, and a popular method used in business and marketing, is to create an Ideal Client Avatar (ICA).

Think of your ideal customer and imagine them in your head. Then create them: give them a name, an age, think of where they live, what their hobbies might be, what their occupation is, what they like to do in their free time, etc. You can draw a picture of them if you'd like! You could even create them as an AI image if you're not an artist. The person you have created is your ICA, and you're going to create your whole book marketing strategy as though you're speaking directly to this person.

See next page for an example of what an ICA might look like and the info you might include:

IDEAL CLIENT AVATAR
(example)

Creating your ICA will help you think clearly about what problems this specific person might have and how you might go about solving them with your book. From a marketing perspective, these points will help determine certain trends that this person might follow, keywords that this person might use in search engines, and categories of interest in which they might fall into—all very helpful information for building adverts too.

Now that you have a clear idea of who your ideal customer is, start gearing your marketing efforts towards that exact person. Maybe you've identified that your avatar loves to practice yoga in their free time. So maybe you seek out the local yoga studios and drop some leaflets or business cards with reception or put a flyer up on a notice board with sales page QR codes and an image of your amazing new book that they need in their life.

Have a think about this first aspect of marketing in relation to your book content. If you've read this section and thought *I need to make some changes to the language in my manuscript!* go do it now before you read any further!

2) *Author Branding and Website*

NOTE: *If you already have an all-singing, all-dancing, branded business website, feel free to skip this step. You can add an author page to your existing website and add sales links to it. This chapter is for people who haven't built a website or a brand before.*

It's not mandatory to have an author website. But it makes you look SUPER professional if you do. People love to be able to 'find' people online, and in the eyes of the consumer, if you're not '*Google-able*', you're not credible.

It doesn't need to be a complicated website—it doesn't even need to be more than one page! Just a simple landing page where people can find out a bit more about you as an author and sales links to your book. At a later stage, you can also set up a direct sales page where customers can buy your book straight through your website from you, rather than through a POD retailer (like Amazon).

If you already have a website for your business, you don't need a new one. The best advice would be to create a new page on your website specifically for your book so people can find it, read more about it, and order it.

Here are some examples of cost-effective, easy-to-use platforms you can use to set up your author website:

- Wix
- Squarespace
- Bluehost
- Groove

If you've never set up a website before, don't have much time available, and aren't hugely tech-minded, Wordpress can be a tricky platform to navigate. It can be quite convoluted and cumbersome compared to other more straightforward platforms out there. However, if you have the time and patience to persist (if you're writing a book and running a business, you may not!), there are some great features and widgets available, and you can build really beautiful websites on Wordpress.

Once you've found a platform to use, you'll need a domain name, which is simply the web address that your website will be connected to.

E.g., ravencrestbooks.co.uk

Domain names can end in .com, .co.uk, .org, .net, as well as other variations. Your website creation platform should be able to supply a free domain name, but it will automatically include the name of the platform.

E.g., ravencrestbooks/wixsite.com

You'll then need to link your domain name to your chosen website platform. You will be able to find instructions on your chosen website platform for how to do this.

Costs

Despite what you might think, the complete costs of setting up and building a website are minimal.

For a basic website, it's not necessary to hire a web designer to do it for you—you can totally do this on your own and save yourself the £200+! Over and above this, it's possible that if you go down the route of hiring a web designer/developer, you then miss out on learning about what has gone on in the backend of your website during its creation. This means that if you ever need to make any changes, you'll end up paying more money to the developer to make those changes for you. And there will always be 'upgrades' that the developer insists need to happen, and if you don't know how to do them yourself, you'll be paying more out of your pocket.

The actual costs for going it alone are:

- Domain name: between £5 and £20 per year (approximately)
- Website platform: this can completely vary on the platform and the package you choose, but you can find very basic packages between £25 and £150 per year

Website Content

For a very basic author website, these three pages are all you really need:

- Home page
- Blog
- Contact me

All three pages will be heavily personalised to your branding, so as soon as a reader lands on your website they get a sense of your vibe, your genre, and what they can expect from your book and from you as an author. We'll get to that in a minute.

Home Page

As far as content goes, the home page might include:

- An introduction/about me paragraph
- Information about your book
- Images/mock-ups of your book
- Sales links and any other relevant links that your reader might be interested in being redirected to

The 'Blog'

Blogging is a crucial aspect of SEO (Search Engine Optimisation) and if you're here as an entrepreneur, you're probably fully aware of what a blog is, what its benefits are, and how painstaking keyword research is! However, for the sake of any new business owners who are here, let's elaborate.

Blogging is a form of content creation used on personal and business websites. The SEO of your website relies heavily on keywords from your blog posts and across your site to boost your visibility and rankings on internet search engines. Blogs or articles are also very useful for giving free information and value to your clients and future readers to build trust. The main thing to focus on when blog-writing is keywords. There is little point in spending hours writing an amazing blog post if the blog doesn't feature keywords relevant to your target audience and your business's content pillars.

Keywords and content pillars link back to your ICA—think of keywords and categories that your dream client might use when searching for a book or service like yours. You can learn plenty more on the topic of SEO from businesses and coaches much better-versed in the subject that you should look up if you want to delve deeper. For now, think of keywords relevant to your ICA and litter them through your blog posts as much as you can (while keeping the content legible and without annoying your readers).

Contact Me Page

Your readers need to know how they can access you. You should include:

- A business email address. A "proper" business email address that matches your web domain name looks much more professional, and you're

more likely to be recognised as a credible author or service provider. Try to avoid setting up a generic email addresses such as hotmail.com and gmail.com.
- Your social media handles
- Potentially a business address if you have one and if it's relevant. People are inherently nosey and like to know whereabouts in the world services are based, so you could include a vague location.

E.g., Shrewsbury, UK.

Now that you have your website set up, you need to think about the branding.

Author Branding

You've already nailed your target audience and created your ICA, so you can start to tailor your brand towards that person. You might think this is a lot of effort to go through to start marketing your book, but this all helps create a solid, believable brand for yourself that people can trust. Just like any aspects of marketing, you can choose to skip this section. But if you've already established from the previous chapter, 'The Self-Publishing Mindset', that you're not just here for your book to collect cobwebs on the Amazon shelves, then let's do this selling-a-book thing properly!

Think about all the brands you see on a day-to-day basis: you probably have a good idea what their company colours are, what the company stands for, what they sell, what their message is, etc. Even if you've never used a particular company for a product, if they have a strong brand, you'll probably know the answers to all the above.

Have a quick search online for other authors or businesses within your niche to check out your peers and competitors' websites.

Notice what colours they use to represent themselves. Bold? Pastels? Bright? Cold? Warm? Is there one main colour throughout the page or do they use a combination of colours that work really well together?

What fonts are they using? Do they use big bold solid fonts? Or do they use light, calligraphic fonts? Is the size of the text large and in your face, or is it in smaller neat paragraphs?

What does the layout look like? Is it a plain, simple white page with an image of the author and the text centre aligned, or is it more haphazard with shapes and arrows that draw your eyes in all directions with many different paragraphs to read? Does the page use imagery?

Think about the emotions evoked by each brand and what vibe the branding gives. Is there a particular use of branding above that makes you more inclined to go there as a consumer? There is no right or wrong answer here. You just need to think creatively about what your ICA would like to see when they land on your homepage, because people definitely *do* judge a book (or anything) by its cover!

To-Do List

- **Build your website**
- **Give it a domain name and connect it to your webpage provider**
- **Set up your domain email address**
- **Write your website content**
- **Nail your website branding with your ICA in mind (remember to keep your branding consistent throughout all platforms)**
- **Add any sales links or "new book coming soon" images**

3) *Social Media*

Love it or hate it, social media is here to stay. New platforms are being developed and launched at an alarming rate, and it can often feel like a huge overwhelm to stay up to date with them all! However, with social media being as popular as it is, implementing it as part of your book marketing strategy is a good choice.

On the flip side, if historically you have struggled with inspiration for social media content creation, your new book is about to give you a whole heap of things to talk about!

An important point to make with social media: try not to overthink or overcomplicate it. As a small business owner, it is impossible to take on the mammoth task of content creation and managing a multitude of social media platforms on top of your daily business to-do list. So don't.

At the very least, pick one and do it really well. Or if you desperately want to have your name or brand across all platforms, hire a social media manager because you are not superhuman and there are only so many hours in the day. Be kind to yourself and work within your means.

But which one to pick? Here are some of your options and some (surprising) user statistics as of January 2024:

- Facebook 3,049 million users

- YouTube 2,491 million users
- Instagram 2,000 million users
- TikTok 1,562 million users
- Snapchat 750 million users
- Twitter 619 million users
- Pinterest 482 million users

(Ref 1)

With Facebook having been around for such a long time, it's surprising to learn that it is still the most popular social media platform. Facebook is very useful for finding niche communities via the Facebook groups option. There are a lot of groups dedicated to book publishing, but it's often hard to separate the wheat from the chaff and you'll sadly find a lot of trolling that often comes from traditionally-published authors pooh-poohing the world of self-publishing.

If you're looking for a friendly, supportive group, you can join the Raven Crest Books 'Build Your Business With A Book' Facebook group. Or if you're a member of our *Self-Publishing Membership*, you have complete access to 'The Self-Publishing Membership Support Group (by Raven Crest Books)'.

Below are the QR codes which will take you to both groups:

When looking for other helpful groups, first check the number of members: too few and they'll be pointless joining; too many suggests a lot of spammy members and your feed will be bombarded with author self-promotion and marketing ploys.

Next, check the volume of group activity. If there's been nothing posted in the last couple of weeks, move on. The most beneficial groups usually have between two and seven posts a day.

Next, you can have a quick scan of what the actual group activity looks like. If the posts are all by the same person (usually the group Admin), then there's clearly not much group engagement and you probably won't learn much or connect with anyone in the group.

Some group headers and keywords to search for in the Facebook group search bar if you're a small business owner wanting to grow their readership are:

- Your business's niche—these groups will be filled with your peers who may be interested in

buying your book but, if not, they will be great for:
- Connecting with—maybe they're writing a book, too, and you can piggyback off each other's audiences
- Learning from—maybe someone has written a book before in your niche
- Recruiting for your ARC team and Beta-Reader team (see page 54)
- Using for editorial reviews (See page 57)
* Groups where your ICA will hang out. For example, if you're a hormone coach, check out the hormone help groups
* Non-fiction writer groups

Once you've found a few valuable groups to join, start engaging regularly.

Pro-Tip: *Don't be a salesperson!*

Community engagement is just as important for your book as it is for your overall business. Here is a phrase which I'm sure you've heard before: people buy from people. People in Facebook groups aren't looking to be sold to, and they already get sold to and cold-messaged on a daily basis so don't be *that* person.

Going straight to the source might seem like the most direct way to approach your potential future clients, but there are warmer ways to engage with your audience and meet their needs.

Spend time on the groups building connections, answering questions, and asking questions too. Be yourself—you may even find that you make some genuine business friends, which is great because they're probably going to be the ones who shout about your book when it's published!

When the time feels right, and an organic opportunity arises to shout about your book, do it! Most groups have specific self-promotion days, so note them down and make the most of them. Here are some organic ways (and not creepy salesman ways) to talk about your book within social media communities:

- **Ask for input**—this might look like: *'I'm currently writing a book and, as you are my target audience, I would* love *your input on my book's title/book cover/topics you'd like to see covered in the book'*. Not only does this provoke engagement, but it also creates an interest in your book and, most importantly, gets your potential readers invested from the start. Imagine how great they'll feel if you use their book cover suggestion. And if people are suggesting things they would like to see covered in your book, they are literally saying to you: *'I have this problem, and I'm desperately looking for an answer to it'*. Your response? *'Thank you so much for your book suggestion. I thought this was a great idea and a common problem that people need solving, so I ended up writing a whole solution-based* *chapter on it!'* Do you think that person might buy your book?

- **Ask which format people like to read**—do members of your target audience prefer an audiobook, an ebook, or do they still like the beauty of holding a physical book in their hands?
- **Ask where people usually get their self-help books/guides/autobiographies from**—Amazon, Waterstones, Barnes & Noble, local bookstores, second-hand shops, library rentals? For example: *'I'm writing a book about ____ and I'm curious to know where you all buy your self-help guides from? Then I'll know where to stock them!'*
- **Any other market research–type questions that are relevant for your niche**—remember to include a sentence reminding everyone that you're writing a book for them! *'As you may know by now, I'm writing a book on ____ and you've been so helpful so far with the market research for it! So, I have one more question:'*
- **Use the poll option** for any of the above talking points—people love an easy interactive experience! You can also utilise this involvement tactic on your Instagram stories.

None of these talking points are salesy at all; in fact, they are the opposite—you're asking other people to help you! But does your target audience now know that you're writing a book especially for them, designed to give answers to all their problems? Yes!

Facebook isn't the only arena where you can implement these techniques. The tips above can be applied across all social media platforms. As mentioned, pick one platform and throw yourself into it. Consistency is key, and you will ideally be posting/commenting in groups/communities/other people's posts one to two times a week to ensure you are becoming a key player in your niche's community.

This section purposefully leaves out general social media content creation, as this needs a whole book in itself—and a social media marketer to write it! The best way to reach your audience is to go directly to them and put the content in front of them rather than creating amazing content for your grid and scratching your head about how to lead your audience to it. The point of this section is to highlight how important social media is for visibility, engagement, community, and connections when used in the right way to market your book.

Takeaways from this section:

- Pick one social media platform and do it well
- Use the fact that you're writing a book to create new content ideas
- Be you
- Be approachable
- Be helpful
- Consistent engagement is key

Which leads very nicely to the next section on mailing lists.

4) Mailing Lists

A mailing list is a list of people who have ever shown an interest in your business, your book, or something you can offer them that you have contact details for. They may have asked to be sent something manually, or they may have signed up to your mailing list via an automation on your website. They may also be a previous or existing client.

It is important to keep track of all email addresses that you accumulate over the span of your business. These email addresses are a direct pathway to your ICAs. And what's more, they're not just cold leads; they are people who have been interested enough in what you do to sign up for something.

IMPORTANT NOTE: *Remember privacy policies when creating an email list. Whether you use a mailing list system, or are keeping track on an excel spreadsheet, you need your GDPR processes up to date to ensure your clients' data is kept private and is not being used for anything they haven't intended it to be used for.*

Mailing lists are key to the launch of your book. As mentioned, your mailing list should be full of people who already fit your ICA bill, so now all you need to do is offer them something they can't live without. And in this case, it's your book. Since your book is designed to answer their problems (some of them—let's not give all your secrets away!), *of course* they need it!

So, how do you generate your mailing list?

The idea of signing up to your mailing list to be amongst the first to hear about your book's launch news might be enough to encourage people to sign up. Otherwise, you may need to be more inventive.

People don't just hand over their email addresses. However, people are generally familiar with the practice of 'subscribing' (entering their email address) to your website in return for a free product/free piece of advice/free solution to their problem/information about new products—generally known as a 'lead magnet'.

Lead magnets are a great way to grow your mailing list because people love getting free stuff. People also hate to miss out on things, so creating a 'sign up to be the first to hear about my latest offers and product discounts' lead magnet is an easy place to start. Simply have this as a small section on your website home page, or as a pop-up.

Here are some non-fiction book-related ideas for lead magnets you can start with (using the nutrition niche as an example) to entice your audience into signing up to your mailing list:

- **Recipes:** Sign up and receive 10 protein-filled breakfast ideas to keep you snack-free until lunchtime
- **Checklists**: Sign up and immediately receive these Top 10 foods to eat to reduce acne

- **Webinars:** Sign up for my free webinar to learn exactly how to track your macros, including macro-tracker program recommendations
- **Challenges:** Sign up for my five-day challenge to reduce your bloat in less than a week!
- **Giveaways:** Sign up now for a chance to win a signed copy of my debut book, plus receive these amazing goodies!

You can talk about these across all your social media platforms, your stories, your podcast, and have them as pop-ups on your website. Remember to include your mailing list link in your social media bios too.

Continuing from the 'Social Media' section, Facebook groups are also a great place to start trying to build your mailing list. Here are some ways you can encourage people who are engaging with your posts on Facebook groups to sign up for your newsletter. But remember, only if they ask you something!

Question: When will your book be launching?

Answer: The launch date hasn't officially been released yet but sign up here (provide the link) and you'll be the first to know!

Question: When will your book cover be revealed?

Answer: Really soon, and I can't wait to show you all. If you like, you can sign up here (provide the link), and you'll be the first to see the cover!

Question: I have this problem (enter problem). Will you address this in your book?

Answer: Yes, but in the meantime, I also have this great freebie that might help answer your query! (Provide link to sign up for freebie.)

As an example, you can also use the Facebook posts to direct people to other parts of your website:

Question: I have this problem (enter problem). Will you address this in your book?

Answer: Yes, but in the meantime, I also have this great blog post that might help you! Sign up to receive weekly blog posts (provide link).

Once you've created your mailing list and started trying to build it, you'll need somewhere to keep track of it. You can simply keep tabs in a good old-fashioned excel spreadsheet. If you're getting people to sign up via your website, then there will automatically be a list created for you on your website platform.

Alternatively, you can use a mailing list platform such as Mailchimp to create email campaigns and manage your customers' information. You can find alternative platforms by searching 'mailing list software' into your search engine.

Now that your mailing list of potential customers is growing, you need to nurture it by engaging with your potential customers. It's important to find the balance of giving your customers enough useful information and offers to keep them interested without driving them towards the *unsubscribe* button with too many spammy emails.

If you already have an established mailing list, please use it for your book promotion! It sounds simple but people often forget about their existing mailing lists when marketing their book. Remember, if people are on your mailing list, they're there because at some point they have been interested in what you offer. And if they no longer want to be there, they will unsubscribe. Don't panic—they may not have fit your ICA anyway. Address the content of your emails directly to your ICA—the ones that are there for the right reasons will appreciate the emails.

Start sending your mailing list teasers, launch dates, cover reveals, and giveaways around two to three months before publication date. Keep reminding them that your book will exist in the world very soon and that anyone who is anyone will be reading it because the book will include [enter juicy content teaser that your audience cannot live without].

Next up, enhance your whole marketing campaign by building a team of cheerleaders who will rave about your book from day one: aka, beta-readers and ARC teams!

5) *Beta-Readers*

An in-depth overview of the beta-reader is covered in the 'Re-Read and Edit' chapter, but this topic has crept into the first marketing chapter for a good reason. Choosing your beta-readers wisely is a key part of your early marketing strategy.

A beta-reader is someone you recruit to be one of the first people to read your manuscript and provide preliminary feedback and improvement points. They can be a professional, someone you know, or someone you don't know. Beta-readers will read the manuscript after you've completed the first round of personal edits. There's nothing stopping you from sending them your very first draft (aka the brain-dump), however you'll probably find that your first draft is so raw it's not worth sending. If you send your first draft, they'll likely only comment on things that you would have corrected yourself if you'd completed an initial read-through. All in all, it's best not to waste your beta-readers on a very first draft.

So why use a beta-reader, and why is this part of your marketing strategy?

It's important to drum up excitement around your book prior to launch day, and what better way to do this than to employ a group of people who tick the boxes of your ICA, who back you and want to help you right from the beginning? People who are literally your ideal audience are perfect to choose for this exercise, as they will be able to offer you improvement points from the perspective of the people who will be buying your book. If you can take your beta-reader's recommendations into account, you should be laughing by the final draft of your manuscript!

Alternatively, you could use a professional beta-reader who will do the job well, create a full report, and give some highly credible and constructive feedback for your book. But picking the right non-professional can really assist with your marketing campaign. And of course, they're getting a free book they would actually read and benefit from, which is great for them too!

Your manuscript at this stage is personal and raw and has come straight from the heart. Trusting someone to read the early stages of your book is a big deal, and the right person will appreciate the responsibility you have given them. Once they have read your manuscript, they will hopefully be invested in the project. Not only will they be able to provide valuable feedback from your ICA's point of view, but they may be keen to hear about how the book turns out, and if you build up a good level of rapport with your beta-readers, the hope is that they will be ideal candidates to shout about your book from the rooftops when it is launched.

So, pick wisely! See page 108 for tips on how to pick a good beta-reader.

6) ARC Team

What is an ARC Team?

The early stages of marketing is the perfect time to start recruiting your ARC team. ARC stands for Advanced Reader Copy, which refers to the copy of your manuscript that you may send to people before the book has officially launched.

In many ways, an ARC team is similar to your beta-reading team, and the two often get confused. However, unlike your crew of beta-readers, your ARC team are not recruited to provide constructive feedback or suggest manuscript improvements; your ARC team are your personal PR and review team. Your beta-readers are involved before the editing process, whereas your ARC team contribute after the book is complete (after your book has been edited, proofread, formatted, and is ready to be uploaded to the POD platforms).

You will send each recruited individual in your ARC team proof copies of your manuscript; this can either be in digital format that they can read on their laptops, tablets, or Kindles, or a physical proof copy you can order for them via your POD platform (see page 169). Bear in mind that physical copies will take longer to arrive, which slows down the process.

As with your beta-reader team, select your ARC team wisely. Choose people who fall into your target audience category, as they'll gain the most value from your manuscript and be more willing to recommend not only your book, but you as a coach or business owner. Furthermore, they might even book you for one-to-one coaching or purchase one of your products or services.

As well as choosing people who meet your ICA criteria, start a second ARC list and look into recruiting high-level professionals or celebrities within your niche. These people are crucial for editorial reviews and endorsements.

What is an editorial review/endorsement?

Editorial reviews are the holy grail of reviews. These are the reviews that come from recognised entities or individuals and that hold the most weight or social proof on your product page. For example, if you were writing a mental health self-help guide, you might send an advanced copy of your manuscript to the head of a leading mental health charity in your country. You might contact a well-known influencer or celebrity mental health ambassador. These are the types of reviews that you'll plaster all over your front covers, much like '*The Sunday Times* – Five Stars' status that you'll see on many books' front covers.

You might also see editorial reviews termed as endorsements. Someone who endorses your book may also be willing to write the foreword for the front matter of your book (see page 128). You may see copy on a book's front cover stating, 'foreword written by ____' and this is only worth including on the front cover if it's written by someone who is recognised in your field and whose name will act as high-level social proof.

The reason the review section is here (we also address reviews at the end of the book in the second marketing chapter on page 234) is that now is the time to start recruiting and collecting email addresses. This way, when your manuscript is complete, all you need to do is get the copies sent out ASAP, rather than enter a last-minute crazed panic about who to send your ARCs to. Being organised means you can make a much better selection for your team.

The other reason is that, whilst you might find it easy to recruit people from your target audience to read and review your book, the likes of influencers, celebrities, and organisations are much harder to get hold of and will likely need a couple of follow-up calls or emails to ensure they're on board.

Pro-Tip: *It's important to note that although your ARC team will hopefully be willing to write you a review that will be published on Amazon post-book launch, you need your editorial reviews and endorsements way before publication date. The idea of editorial reviews is to use them as social proof to attract people to buy your book, so you will need these reviews in time to use quotes on your marketing material and even on your front cover. Therefore, be* *clear of your deadlines when you contact people asking for reviews.*

What do I say when recruiting my ARC team?

Here's the catch: whilst the idea of asking for reviews and receiving them might seem like an easy task, Amazon doesn't actually like you to ask for reviews. If they think you have purposefully swapped a free book in return for a review, they won't be too happy about it.

From their perspective, you can see how it might look like bribery, which is against their review policy.

Therefore, obtaining reviews the right way comes down to how you word the communication to your ARC team. You might say something like this:

Thank you for agreeing to be part of the ARC team for my debut book, launching on _____. This is such a key part of my book launch, and I'm so grateful for everyone who agreed to be on my team, helping to drive the excitement about my book.

I will be sending you a proof copy of the book by the [insert date]. I ask that in return for me sending you a free advanced copy of my manuscript, you ensure to have read it by the [insert date that falls before launch day].

Whilst you are reading, if you come across any typos or spelling mistakes, I ask that you report them to me immediately so I can get these amended before the official launch.

Other than this, I really hope you like the book and find it valuable and can't wait to hear what you think!

If you love the book (which I hope you do!), you are more than welcome to leave an honest review on Amazon or Goodreads on or after the publication date. If you have any social media accounts, I would be forever grateful if you share your thoughts with your followers too.

The other marketing chapter at the end of this book goes into more detail on the review process and about following up with your ARC team (see page 232).

Oh, and remember to ask your ARC team if they'd like to be added to your mailing list for future offers, services, and giveaways!

To-Do List

- **Start creating your ARC team by:**
    - **Contacting people you know who fall into your ICA specification**
    - **Search and network with new people who fit your ICA bill**
- **Make a note of their contact details**
- **Give them plenty of info and keep in contact with them throughout the process**

7) PR

PR (Public Relations) is an aspect of personal brand promotion that falls under the umbrella of marketing. PR is responsible for how you (and your book) come across to the public.

Finding relevant contacts for your book's PR is very closely linked to the kind of people you might be thinking about contacting for editorial reviews. Essentially, you want everyone to know about your book and you want your book to have exposure; if your book has exposure, so do you and your business, and isn't that what this is all for?

How does your book get exposure? Through you, the author, making connections and landing PR opportunities with as many media platforms as possible. Big-time book PR relies heavily on media outlets to boost the exposure of the author to, in turn, sell books.

This is not to say that, just because you're writing a book, *This Morning* or *The Late Show* are going to get in touch and request an interview with you that leads to a million-pound book deal with Penguin Random House. But if you don't put yourself out there, you'll never know.

Make sure you choose the relevant people within the business to contact, i.e., make sure you are contacting editors and content advisors, not the costume department or customer service teams.

The PR List

At this stage, all you need to think about is creating a PR contact list. The actual content of your press release will come later, and here's why:

You don't want to contact the media Big Dogs without a mock-up image of your book attached, as your press release won't look professional enough and your application may not even make it past the gatekeepers. You'll need at least a front cover, if not a full sleeve, before sending out your press release. For this reason, the creation of your press release is addressed later in the book on page 227.

For your PR list, make a list of all the media platforms you can think of that might potentially offer you an interview, appearance, or some sort of exposure. Think of TV shows, newspapers, magazines, radio shows, and podcasts. Do not underestimate the effectiveness of podcasts as part of your book's PR strategy. Podcasts are currently hugely popular and it's a wise choice to utilise them for exposure for you and your book.

Do your research, find the relevant podcasts, TV shows, radio shows, newspapers, and magazines—ideally the ones where the listeners and viewers are your ICAs—and find the appropriate contacts. Read about what to include in your book's press release on page 227.

If you're following along with the *Self-Publishing Membership* course, you can find a visual example of a book press release in the 'PR' module.

Once you have generated your list, it's time to get Googling to find the right contacts for the right people. People are so accessible these days that it's easier than you think to get in touch with celebrities and big names that you might previously have thought of as being completely unreachable. If you're contacting TV shows, newspapers, and magazines, ensure you look for the editors' details. If you're contacting celebrities, search for their agents. Remember, agents *want* to be found for bookings, so they don't make it difficult.

8) *Podcasts*

The online scene is littered with podcasts at the moment; the world has gone podcast crazy. We're a society that's constantly "too busy" to do anything, so the accessibility of being able to listen to a podcast on-the-go has become very alluring to the mass population.

Hence, this is a great platform for you to explore to reach new and ready-made audiences.

Spend some time researching podcasts and make sure the podcast has a decent enough following so it's worth your while. A lot of podcast hosts also broadcast their podcasts in video form on YouTube, so check to see if they have a reasonable number of subscribers on YouTube too.

You will want to start applying for podcast guest slots as early as possible—a lot of shows get booked up with guests pretty far in advance, especially the popular ones. Not only that, but they will often record the sessions months before they go live, so make sure to ask the podcast host when they plan to air your episode. Try to request to appear on an episode around your launch date or within the three weeks following your book's publication.

The bigger podcasts usually have their own websites through which you can contact the hosts about guest appearances. When you do get offered that guest feature slot, ask for the opportunity to sell yourself and plug your book.

Whilst this book specifically addresses book marketing, these are all tools and methods you can apply to your actual business's marketing strategy if you don't already. You're welcome!

You should start to see by now why writing a book to build your business is such a good idea—a book really gives you something to shout about, as well as other people a reason to talk about you. Look at the exposure your business is getting!

Chapter 5
Create Your Publishing Timeline

Now that you've got an idea of what the early stages of marketing looks like, it's the perfect time to put a publishing timeline together. This is especially important when using your book to market your business; you may need to consider business forecasting to make sure you have the right amount of money available at the right time. It's also important if you have a specific time at which you want to launch your book. For example, if your book is a mental health self-help guide, you may want to launch your book during National Mental Health Week. This event may be two months away or it may be four months away, so plan your timeline accordingly. Or maybe you want to plan the launch of your book with the promotion of a new service you're offering so, again, organisation is key.

This section will give you an idea of the timeframes involved when launching a book.

You'll need to take your own personal workload into consideration. So, if you know that, three weeks from now, you are going away for a week-long business event or a holiday and won't be doing any work on your book during this time, plan around this. The timeframes in this section will be based on self-publishing your book around a part-time/flexible work schedule.

Once you've mapped out the publishing process and know when your book launch is going to be, you can then work backwards and slot the key marketing aspects into your plan. Book marketing ought to fit in around other aspects of book publishing, as marketing is an ongoing task.

You might have software you can use to map out your book publishing timeline; you may want to use trusty Excel; or, you could even stick to good old-fashioned pen and paper and create an aesthetically pleasing graph that you can stick on your office wall.

When using this book to put a timeline together, you can choose to read the full book first—so you're aware of what is involved during each part of publishing—then return to this section to put a timeline together, or you can put a timeline together based on the following timeframes, then use the book as a step-by-step guide as you publish.

You'll find the timeframes noted in ranges below, but the recommendation would be to take the maximum timeframe to allow for any of the processes taking longer than expected.

Pro-Tip: *If you're booking a freelancer who is particularly sought-after, they may need securing two to three months in advance, maybe even longer.*

If you have your heart set on a particular freelancer, book them early.

These are all based on an average book length of 70–80,000 words, so if your book is shorter, it is possible that aspects such as editing, formatting, and proofreading will be completed more quickly than indicated. Remember that each of these aspects of publishing will be addressed in detail throughout the book, so don't panic if you're seeing some unfamiliar words at this stage!

- **Marketing:** Ongoing throughout—ideally to begin minimum 12 weeks before launch. This can start whilst you are still writing your first draft.
- **Cover design:**
    - **Self-publishing:** 1–2 weeks
    - **If outsourcing:** 2–8 weeks. Start this process early, too! Again, this can be started before you've finished your first draft.
- **Beta-readers:** Allow them 2–3 weeks to read and provide feedback, especially if you've enlisted someone for free.
- **Editing:**
    - **Self-publishing:** 1–2 weeks
    - **If outsourcing:** 1–4 weeks (Plus 1 week post-editing to go through and accept/reject changes and make any final amends you might want to make)

- **Proofreading:**
  - **Self-publishing:** 1 week
  - **If outsourcing:** 1–2 weeks
- **Formatting:**
  - **Self-publishing:** 1–2 weeks. If it's taking you longer, outsource!
  - **If outsourcing:** 1–2 weeks
- **POD platform management** (from upload to hitting 'publish'): 1 week
  - **If ordering and approving proof copies:** 1–4 weeks
- *(Optional)* **Recommended time between formatting completion and hitting 'publish' to ensure you stand the best chance of marketing your book and obtaining reviews, endorsements, and quotes before publication:** 4–8 weeks.

Based on the above timeframes, if completely self-publishing (not relying on external contractors), you can easily publish a book to a high standard in less than 12 weeks when following the steps in this book. Marketing your book will take longer and is such a crucial aspect of your book's future success. So, consider that marketing your book will add on a couple of months to your timeframe if you want your book to succeed.

The complete order of your timeline, including marketing, might look like this (remember this is based on having a first draft complete, or near completion):

Month 1:
Start the 'early marketing' as per Chapter 4: establish your beta-readers, create your PR list
Start the cover design process
Finish your first draft and write your 'extra copy'

Month 2:
Send your MS to your beta-readers
Finish your own edits
Send MS to an editor
Finish cover design
Create press release
Send press release to PR list for PR opportunities and book endorsements
Keep your audience updated on your book's progress on social media

Month 3:
Receive edited MS from editor and self-review it
Send to proofreader when happy with MS
Start the formatting process
Start sharing book mock-ups to generate excitement on social media
Secure PR opportunities and endorsement requests and follow up on PR opportunities and endorsement requests who haven't replied (repeat this every two weeks)

Month 4:
Complete formatting
Send the formatted MS to your ARC team
Upload your MS and book covers to your POD platform and complete the POD set-up

Create your A+ content
Order proof copies

Month 5:
Review and approve proof copies; make any MS amends as required
Use mailshots and social media to run giveaways, keep audience updated, and generally promote the launch of your book
Keep up communication with your ARC team and PR efforts
Launch your book!

Month 6:
Ongoing post-launch marketing

This is a rough guide. There are more marketing tools you can scatter strategically into this timeline too (as documented in Chapters 4 and 12)—you'll know what's right for your business and your schedule—but hopefully this gives you an excellent starting point.

Chapter 6
Write a Sales-Converting Back Cover Blurb

The back cover description, or 'book blurb', is the second part of your sales pitch after your front cover.

Once your amazing cover has attracted the reader's attention, the next part of the reader's journey is to flip to the back cover to see what the book is about. If your readers are picking up a physical copy of your book, this is where the blurb will be. If your reader is purchasing via an online platform, the book blurb often doubles as the book description on the sales page (but can be different).

It's important for your book's cover to convey an accurate representation of the book's description, because if the two aren't aligned, then your reader will quickly put the book back on the shelf.

It's kind of stressful to try and summarise your whole book into one or two paragraphs. There's a lot of pressure riding on this text! A successful book blurb should entice the reader into wanting to read more. If it gives too much or too little away, you may turn the reader off.

The first sentence is crucial. Imagine it like the first line of a catchy advert you've seen on TV. If the delivery of the first sentence on an advert is successful, your ears will prick up. You'll watch the whole ad, which will potentially result in you purchasing whatever they are selling. If the ad is weak, *maybe* something in the middle of the ad will grab your attention, but twenty-first-century humans have a very short attention span, so you need to draw in your audience within the first line of your description.

When writing a non-fiction book, guide, or memoir, think about:

- What are the reader's pain points?
- What value is your book providing to your reader?
- What questions are you answering for them?
- What problem can they expect to solve by reading this book?
- What is your overriding message?
- Who is the book written for/to?
- What is your book's USP (Unique Selling Point)?

If you can nail the above points, this will be the difference between someone buying your book, or scrolling to the next one.

If you've ever had any coaching from a marketing consultant or business coach on writing sales copy, whether it's for social media or landing pages on your website, writing a back cover blurb for your non-fiction book will probably take a very similar process. All the above points apply to both.

When referring to pain points, this means get into the reader's head and think deeply about the problem they have that has brought them in search of your book. But don't just name the problem, *feel* the problem.

Let's use an example of a reader searching for a book on hormone health. The reader has a history of hormone disruption and is looking for answers to improve their life.

The problem: Disruptive hormones leading to a decline in their overall state of wellness.

The feelings: Miserable that their day-to-day happiness is being compromised. Frustrated that after searching high and low, they can't find the answers they need. Sad and outcast; feeling like the only person going through this problem.

The blurb: *Realising your happiness (or lack of) is being dictated by your hormones can be frustrating. Especially if you've investigated various avenues and reached multiple dead ends in your research.*

Doctors are fobbing you off, and you're sick of test results coming back as 'normal' when you feel anything BUT normal! If you're tired of feeling miserable about your compromised hormone health and are ready to take action, this book is here to provide the answers.

As a coach, your job is to provide solutions to peoples' problems and to guide them on their journey to their desired outcome. You're a problem-solver by nature, so make sure your blurb highlights this. Ensure you let your reader know in the blurb exactly what problems your book is going to solve. How will the reader feel when they've reached the end of your book? What can they expect to achieve? How can they expect to feel?

It should be obvious from your blurb who the book is written for. You don't need to divulge this information specifically but direct your language towards your ICA. Or you could really call a spade a spade and speak exactly to your people by writing something like:

Are you a woman tortured by terrible hormone health and desperate to find answers?

Get creative but also look at your competitors' book blurbs for inspiration. Obviously don't copy them—for one, that blurb already exists, and two, they're not you. And three, that's not cool.

Chapter 7
Design an Eye-Catching Book Cover

1. Demographic and Research
2. Images, Stock Photos, and Licences
3. Typography
4. The Back Cover and Full Sleeve
5. Sizing
6. Print Standards
7. Hiring a Designer and Buying Premade

A book cover can make or break your book. Your book cover is literally your initial sales pitch to the world. Most people will pick a book off the 'shelf' (real or virtual) purely based on the cover. Yup, despite repeatedly being told not to, we humans are literally judging books by their covers every single day.

It needs to be eye-catching, but it also needs to represent your book honestly and not mislead readers. There is no point in your book cover being amazing but attracting the wrong audience. This could lead to bad reviews or low page reads on Kindle Unlimited (see page 218), which we'll come to later, but in a nutshell, a misleading cover is not good for royalties.

If you have artistic flair and a keen eye for graphic design, there is absolutely nothing stopping you from designing the cover yourself. Even if you plan to outsource this aspect of self-publishing, if you have an idea in your head of how you want your cover to look, creating a mock-up design to send to the designer is a good move to make sure you effectively get your ideas across.

We'll get to hiring designers later in the chapter. For now, let's assume you're going to have a go yourself. Good on you! Read the next seven sections thoroughly and your cover will be in good hands.

As far as timeline is concerned, the cover design needs to happen so early in the process for these reasons:

- If you're outsourcing, the design process can be very back and forth to make sure the end product is something you love. It can therefore take up a reasonable chunk of the timeline
- If you're learning how to create a cover yourself, this can be an equally long-winded task
- The earlier you have your book cover ready, the earlier you can start creating book mock-ups and start marketing
- If you have your front cover complete, you can start your ebook pre-order (more pre-order info on page 200).

1) *Demographic and Research*

Research

Before starting your book cover design, you *must* research book covers in your genre. You'll find that each genre will have a book cover design formula that most authors within the genre tend to follow.

For example, you'll probably find that crime thriller books have dark, creepy backgrounds, bold red or yellow lettering for the title, and contrasting white typography for the author's name.

For romantic comedies, using vector-style imagery (computer-made illustrative designs) is common along with calligraphic typography.

Non-fiction books tend to be more word-heavy with bold typography on a plain backdrop.

The point is, you can usually tell a book's genre from its cover. Designers use these winning formulas because they work. And if it ain't broke, don't fix it.

First things first, jump on Amazon and check out the non-fiction categories. Better still, work out the specific category your book will fall into and see what kind of design formula your competitors are using. Check out your category's best-selling covers too.

This is also a good way to make sure your book title doesn't already exist! Often in non-fiction, many books contain quite similar content. Take books about menopause, for example—the factual scientific content may remain the same across each book; the difference comes from the writer's style of writing, their angle on the subject determining the type of solutions they provide, and the audience they're targeting. (Other than the obvious 40-plus-year-old women!)

This often means that titles used for a specific niche won't vary much. How can you make your book stand out from the crowd? Stay away from the obvious unimaginative titles such as:

- A Guide to Menopause
- Menopause: The Survival Kit
- How to Combat Menopause
- Health Tips for Women Over 40

On the flip side, these titles are great for your book's keyword optimisation (how Amazon indexes your book), as it's very clear what they offer.

Using a play on words is a fun idea when naming your book. But if the title itself doesn't obviously portray what the book might be about, make sure the subtitle really drills home the book's subject and includes relevant keywords to tick the SEO box. Two great examples of more interesting book titles in the menopause genre are Davina McCall's 'Menopausing' and Bryony Gordon's 'Mad Woman'.

Get creative, get inspired!

Back to cover design. When you're scrolling through Amazon for book cover ideas, look out for:

- Quality
- Fonts used
- Image type (vector, photos, illustration, etc.)
- Design layout (image-to-word ratio, how many words are used, how big the author's name is compared to the title, where on the page the title is)
- Subtitles
- Colours used

You can explore outside of Amazon too. Have a look through the Waterstones website, or if you're in the US, Barnes & Noble. Make notes. Wander around your local bookstore, create a mood board, do whatever you need to make sure you gather enough information about how to make your book cover look amazing whilst staying true to your genre.

Demographic

Research complete, now you need to nail meeting your demographic's needs. Refer back to the ICA you created in the first 'Marketing' chapter (page 30). Design your book cover as if you are creating it just for your ICA. What book can you imagine them already reading? What To-Be-Reads do they have waiting on their bedside table? Which books are going to jump out at them at a bookstore and why? What is it about those particular books that have drawn them in?

Which design software should I use?

There are some great accessible programs on the market currently—paid and free. Amazon KDP does have its own free cover design tool, but the outcome of using this tool will likely be far from professional.

A great free graphic design platform on the market currently is Canva. Adobe products are also popular among cover designers but are not free.

You can create some great graphics on Canva using photos, high-resolution stock images, your own images, and various creative fonts, filters, and editing tools. There are even book cover templates available you can use to give you a starting point and some inspiration. You may find the free version limiting, but the pro version is inexpensive and it provides a much wider variety of image options.

Pro-Tip: *If you end up choosing to use a book cover template, please edit and re-create it so it's not recognisable as a generic Canva template and it is your own work. Firstly, to legally protect yourself* *and secondly, imagine going on Amazon after your launch and seeing your exact book cover had already been used by a different author.*

Adobe products are designed to be a graphic-designer's go-to tools. They are the market-leading one-stop-shop *(Ref 8)*. But the tool is only as good as the person using it, and Adobe products aren't free. You'll also need to spend a fair bit of time learning how navigate the software before you can start creating your cover. As with all Adobe packages, they are not initially very user-friendly and are designed for professionals who have been trained to use the specific software day in, day out. They are not intended for hobbyists or people who plan on creating one design a year.

Having said all this, you can create some beautiful designs with InDesign, Illustrator, and Photoshop if you know how to use them. So, if you are looking to invest in a more high-end graphic design platform, make sure you also devote enough time to spend learning how to use it to its ultimate potential. Otherwise, you will have wasted your money.

<u>To-Do List</u>

- **Find a design software to use**
- **Do your market research**
- **Always meet your ICA's needs**

2) *Images, Stock Photos, and Licences*

When it comes to choosing the images you want to use on your book's cover, there are some things you should know about the legalities of using specific images.

The easiest way to use an image on your cover is if you design it or take the photo yourself. The image copyright remains with the image owner, which would be you. You can also reach out to a photographer and pay them a fee to take the exact photo you want and document in writing that the image rights will remain with you, rather than the photographer.

Canva allows you to use its images for commercial and non-commercial use, which is great (*Ref 9*—you can read further Canva licensing information here).

The complications arise when searching for images from the internet. For example, you cannot simply search for an image in Google Images and proceed to use it on your cover without obtaining permission from the copyright owner. You would need to track down the image owner and obtain a licence for that particular image. The other issue is that if you were to simply save a photo from Google Images, the quality would be extremely low resolution! So just don't do it. (See Glossary for what constitutes 'high resolution'.)

Luckily, you'll find plenty of stock image websites online where you can download the exact high-resolution images you require. You can usually pay for images separately, or if you know you're going to need regular access to image downloads, you can sign up for a monthly subscription.

Whichever site you end up choosing for your stock images, read the licensing policies. Depending on how you are planning on using the image you purchase, some licences only allow up to a certain number of commercial products to be produced using one particular image. Some platforms allow unlimited product production, but book covers are often excluded from this clause. If you come across this, there is usually an advanced licence or pro licence you'll need to buy which will then allow you access to what you need. This additional licence can often cost around £100 on top of what you've already paid to purchase the image. As you can see, the costs can really start stacking up! And you can see why cover designers charge what they do.

Generally, if you're not expecting to sell more than 100,000 copies of your book, you'll probably be safe from the more expensive licensing fees. But if you're shooting for the big numbers, be mindful of what's included in the licence clauses.

Some of the most popular image stockists that you should check out in 2024 are *(Ref 10):*

- Shutterstock
- Adobe Stick
- Vecteezy
- Unsplash
- Deposit Photos
- Flickr

Pro-Tip: *If you're hiring a cover designer, they should incorporate the cost of any images they use into their price. But make sure you clarify this with the designer to avoid any surprises on receipt of their invoice.*

Using images on your book cover

Once you have chosen which platform you're going to obtain your high-resolution images from, you need to decide which images you're going to use. Think back to the demographic section and who your audience is.

Non-fiction books are typically text-heavy, but that's not to say you'll never see imagery used. It's not uncommon for people to use a photo of themselves on the front cover of autobiographies or memoirs. You could use a plain, non-fussy background, or you can consider using a simple image that represents the message in your book—objects that hold strong metaphorical value, such as mountains, flowers, icebergs, etc.

Think about the colours used in your image and what the colours represent. As mentioned in the demographic section, if your book is warm and emotional, choose warm, inviting colours. If your book is factual and straight to the point, you might opt for cooler colours.

If you are using an image for your cover background, it's important to choose an image that doesn't use too many different colours. If your background image incorporates a wide variety of colours, it'll be tricky to find a font colour that stands out from the background.

Remember, your cover design does not need to be fancy and technical. You don't need to hone your Photoshop skills to chop out backgrounds and blend objects together. Your design simply needs to:

- Be eye-catching
- Be relevant to and represent your content
- Appeal to your ICA
- Have clear messaging
- Be legible

NOTE: *When thinking about your cover background, remember you have a back cover to design too. The entire book cover (including the spine) is called the sleeve. A lot of books have one big image spread across the whole sleeve. Some have one image but a different spine, breaking it up. And* *some have a different image or background colour on each aspect of the cover. See the 'Sizing' section on page 94 for more on the full sleeve.*

To-Do List

- **Use high-resolution images only**
- **Read the small print on licensing when purchasing your images**
- **Don't forget your back cover!**

3) *Typography*

This is a posh word meaning the words on your front cover. Typography incorporates every aspect of how the text on your cover looks; the size, colour, font, orientation, placement, texture, etc.

Make sure you choose a font that goes well with the image or background you've used for your cover and a colour that stands out. For example, if you've used a dark blue background, don't use a black for your font.

Think about the alignment of your font, i.e., where you want it positioned on the page.

Right
aligned?

Left
Aligned?

        Or maybe centred.

    Or maybe
        You just want it
            A bit all over
                The place

There is no right or wrong answer; you'll know what is right for your book.

Are you going to use the same font for each word? Or will you mix up the smaller words with slightly different fonts?

Maybe
Something
Like
This

Will all the letters be the same size? Or is there a prominent letter in the title that perhaps needs accentuating?

Can you do something clever with any of the letters—can you turn the dot on the 'i' into something; an apple if you're a nutritionist or a lotus flower if you're a mindfulness expert. Can you turn the tail of a 'g' into a cat's tail if you're a… a cat therapist. Anyway, you get the point!

Think about the other text you might have on your front cover too. Where do you want your name to go? Will you use a different font? Or a different colour? Or both? If you get an amazing editorial review, where will you position this? Do you need a subtitle to make it completely obvious to your readers what your book is about? And don't forget the back cover text! There is more info about the back cover in the next section on (page 91).

Bet you never thought there was so much going on with the text on a book cover! Is your creative brain inspired yet? Time for you to get those ideas down and get designing!

4) *The Back Cover and Full Sleeve*

When creating your full sleeve, you need to think about the aesthetics of the back cover if you plan to print your book as a paperback or hardback. You do not need a back cover if you are just producing an eBook. For the purpose of this book, 'full sleeve' is referenced in the simplest form as the incorporation of the front and back covers, along with the spine, without any flaps or dust jacket.

Have a look at some books and notice the different styles of sleeve arrangement. Some books have one image that covers the whole spread. Some books have the same image across the full sleeve, but a different spine design. Some books use one image that runs across the front cover and spine but use a different image or background colour for the back cover. And some books have completely different styles across all three elements of the sleeve.

The same design aspects apply to the back cover as discussed in previous sections about the front cover, although there is obviously less room for creativity. The back cover is home to your book blurb. Bear in mind how long your blurb is and how big the space is on your cover. If you know your blurb is bulky, leave enough room for the text when you're designing it.

Your back cover needs to showcase your blurb. As mentioned in the 'Write Your Back Cover Blurb' chapter (page 72), this text is your chance to sell your book. And having nailed the copy, you need to make sure your audience can read it clearly. Ensure the colour of your font contrasts nicely with the background colour/image. If you're finding it hard to find a font colour that stands out against your background image, don't be afraid to experiment with different-shaped and different-coloured text boxes to insert your blurb into. These can be completely opaque to ensure the highest level of legibility, or translucent so as not to impose on the overall feel of the book.

Decide whether you want to include a photo of yourself on the back cover. Author photos are often displayed on the back cover or sometimes within the 'About the Author' section (See page 132). If you decide to include a photo of yourself, think about placement of the image and where it looks best.

Make sure the self-portrait used is high resolution—you'll ruin your whole cover and the authority of your work if your author image is pixelated.

Leave room for the barcode when you're designing the back cover. If you're using KDP cover calculator (described in the 'Sizing' section on page 94), the barcode is included so you can see clearly how to avoid overlapping it.

If you're not using a template, remember to leave an approximate gap for it on the bottom right corner of your back cover. The barcode should be a minimum of 20mm high by 30mm wide (*Ref 13*). You can preview your cover on the POD platforms before you publish. The preview shows you where the barcode will appear on publication. If the barcode is overlapping any important information on your back cover, make any necessary amends before publishing.

5) *Sizing*

Paperback and Hardback format

As mentioned, 'full sleeve' refers to the complete jacket of your book, comprised of three elements: the front cover, the spine, and the back cover.

Sizing your full sleeve can be a pain but, with the help of using a template, your life will become a lot easier. If you have a KDP account (even if you choose not to publish on KDP), there is a handy cover calculator you can use to work out the exact dimensions you require to size your cover accurately. You'll need this info when creating the template:

- Binding type (paperback or hardback)
- Interior type (black and white or colour)
- Paper type (cream or white)
- Page turn direction*
- Measurement units
- Interior trim size (this is the paper size you used to format your manuscript to, i.e., 5 x 8 inches)
- Page count

*The direction you plan for the reader to turn the pages in your book. For standard western formatting, the answer is left to right.

Because of the last bullet point, you can only accurately complete the sizing of your book cover after the formatting is complete. Only when formatting is complete will you know exactly how many pages your book will be, and only then can you produce a template on KDP. But start your design now—designing your cover after formatting is complete is too late! You can make minor adjustments to your completed cover once you have your template.

NOTE: *Don't get the cover calculator tool confused with the KDP cover creator tool. The cover calculator template generator is a separate item that you can download and this is the one you need.* (See page 196 in the content section in KDP set-up for navigation to the template).

Your chosen POD platform will flag errors such as images or text falling outside of the margins on the template. Following the KDP template accurately should stop these errors occurring.

If you're following along with *The Self-Publishing Membership* course material, the video in the 'Book Cover Design' module shows exactly how to find and generate a book cover template on KDP which you can use when creating your book cover.

Book size is important, as it adds to the whole feel of the completed book. Most books tend to be approximately 5 x 8 inches, but another popular POD size is 6 x 9 inches. It's really down to preference and what size you think your ICA would prefer to hold in their hand, as well as which looks better.

Sizing can also be tactical; if your book is too long and you want to minimise your print costs, you could choose 6 x 9 to bring your page count down. On the flip side, if you want your book to achieve the look of having more content than it does, choose 5 x 8 inches. The more pages your book has, the higher your printing costs will be.

Pro-Tip: *Remember which size you've chosen when it comes to cover design, so you can size your interior to the same dimensions.*

eBook

The eBook cover sizing process is much more straightforward. The online upload only requires the front page of your cover. Simply resize your front page to your chosen book size in whichever platform you are using to create your cover. Save it as a JPG or PNG file. When you've finished with the book cover design phase, you should have one full sleeve image and one front cover image saved.

Pro-Tip: *You may find it helpful to have the back cover and the spine saved as individual files too. This will come in handy when creating book mock-ups for promo graphics to market your book.*

6) *Print Standards*

Finishing your complete product to a high standard is so important. It cannot be stressed enough that if the end product is poor quality, the content of your book will be viewed less reputably.

If your cover design's quality is too low (i.e., pixelated/not high-resolution enough), this will likely be flagged by your POD platform anyway. But if you have followed the guidelines in the previous cover creation sections then hopefully you'll have produced a beautiful, high-quality book cover.

Now for the finishing touches.

You're probably going to be using a POD company to print your book, and whilst the quality of POD is extremely good, it's not going to match the high-end quality of an offset printer (see page 212 for information on printing). Therefore, it's important to finish the overall book production to the highest standard possible while *you* are in control of things, before you hand it to the POD printers.

Ticking the right boxes to ensure your book is well-finished is an easy task, so make sure you tick them!

Interior printing

To ensure your interior gets printed to a high standard, saving your formatted manuscript in PDF-x1a format is recommended. Saving in this format means that your manuscript will be printed in the exact way it was saved. The conversion of the file creates this outcome by all sorts of complicated embedding and flattening processes, which is too technical to need to know about for the purpose of self-publishing!

Raven Crest Books has previously experimented with different print formats, and the difference between printing a book using a PDF Standard interior versus a PDF-x1a interior is vast.

You can convert your file to this format using an online file converter. Simply type 'file converter PDF-x1a' into your search engine.

For additional guidance, check out the video in the 'Technical Stuff' module in *The Self-Publishing Membership* for a tutorial on how to convert and save your manuscript in this format.

Cover Printing

The cover ideally needs to be produced in the same format (PDF-x1a). If whichever platform you are using to create your cover won't let you save your file directly as a PDF-x1a file (for example, you can't do this in Canva), instead download/save your file as high quality as possible. This will usually be PDF Print CMYK (Cyan, Magenta, Yellow, and Key) for optimum colour availability. From here, you can then use a file conversion platform to convert the file to a PDF-x1a file.

7) *Hiring a Designer and Buying Premade*

If your creativity lies elsewhere or you have no interest in creating and designing your own cover, you can always outsource this part of your book's production. There is no need to feel ashamed for outsourcing—recognising where you require help in a project is a great skill to have.

Hiring a Designer

Here are some reasons you might think about hiring a designer rather than going it alone:

- Your creativity lies elsewhere
- You recognise that there are professionals better suited for the task
- You don't know anyone who has design skills who could do this for you
- You have the budget to hire a designer
- You don't have time to design your own cover
- You have big goals for your book, aiming for it to be hugely successful and need a cover that will enable you to accomplish your goals

You can find more information about hiring a trustworthy designer in the *Hiring a Freelancer* chapter (page 19). Here are some things you should have ready to send over when working with a designer on your book cover.

- A cover brief, detailing:
  - Your target audience
  - Book synopsis (so the artist can get a feel for the book's content)
  - General ideas for what you want your cover to look like
  - The message you want your cover to convey
  - Colour ideas
  - Font ideas (Bold, narrow, round, calligraphic, italic, sans serif, etc.)
  - Imagery ideas
  - Text you want on the front cover (title, subtitle, author name, quotes, etc.)
  - Text you want on the back cover (book blurb, quotes, reviews)
  - A photo of you, if you want it included on the back cover
- Attach images of book covers that you like (take screen shots of existing books in your genre online)
- Any doodles/visuals you can produce to get your idea across fully
- Your timeframe/deadline

You will also need to ask the designer to outline exactly what is included in the cover design service they are providing:

- How many initial concepts will they send over? (Some designers only include one idea, and if

you don't like that idea—providing they have stuck to your brief—you'll have to pay for another concept delivery.)
- Do they include unlimited revisions before publication?
- Do they include changes to the cover post-publication? (For example, if you have an editorial review to add to the front cover or you've added content to the interior and therefore the spine size needs changing.) And if so, for how long after post-publication?
- If any of the above are not included in the initial rate, what are the additional charges?

Hiring a designer for your book cover can be expensive. And they deserve to be—the good ones are extremely talented!

It's tricky to comment on how much hiring a designer will cost you, because cost is completely dependent on the experience of the designer, their pricing strategy, and the complexity of the design you are asking for. Generally speaking, you can expect to pay anything from £150 to £2,000.

The best thing you can do is to get online, get recommendations, find some designers whose work you like, and start asking around for prices to help align your expectations with your budget.

It's worth keeping in mind that the best designers often have a waiting list (as with other freelancers, too). So, when choosing your designer, always ask them how long they think it will take to finish your project and work this into your publishing timeline.

Premade Covers

These are essentially an easy way for a cover designer to make passive income. They will have created hundreds of premade designs and uploaded them to their website. Authors can then go along and pick one. The designer will either send you the template to personalise or complete it for you and ta-da! Cover complete.

Depending on the experience of the designer and the quality of the work, you can usually expect to pay between £90 and £300 for a premade cover, but generally, buying a premade cover is cheaper than paying for a bespoke cover design service.

Pro-Tip: *If you go for this option, please make sure that your designer is planning to take your chosen design off the shelf once you have bought it, otherwise chances are you may see your exact design under another author's name the next week. Not the best look!*

To find a premade cover for your book, just search 'premade book covers' on your online search engine.

You can also check out 99 Designs for book covers where you can advertise your job and designers will bid for the project.

Chapter 8
The Re-Read and Edit

1. Re-Reading Your Manuscript
2. Beta-Readers/Manuscript Review
3. Hiring an Editor
4. Different Types of Editing
5. Proofreading
6. Extra Copy
7. ISBNs

Time to get to the nitty-gritty part of book publishing: perfecting the actual content. It may surprise you that you are only getting down and dirty with the edits in Chapter 8, near the end of the book! There really is *so* much more to self-publishing than people often think.

The editing phase all starts with the completely unglamorous re-read of your whole manuscript. But this part is so crucial! Read on to find out why.

1) *Re-Reading Your Manuscript*

Let me start by explaining what the term 'first draft' (or 'initial draft') actually represents. A first draft is basically a 'brain-dump' of your ideas onto paper. It's usually unfiltered, unstructured, undignified—even uninteresting! A first draft is exactly what it says on the tin, and an editor or publisher should never lay their eyes on this stage of your MS. The first draft is for your eyes only.

Imagine a theatre group doing an initial run-through of a new script and announcing after the first practice, 'Right guys, I think we're ready for an audience!' You're practically inviting negative comments and feedback into your life, completely unnecessarily.

That's essentially what you're doing when you submit a first draft to an editor or publisher.

What you *do* want to submit to an editor or publisher is a 'final draft'. A final draft is a document that has been re-read, had a couple of rounds of tweaks and edits completed by the author, and has even been reviewed by your peers. (I'll get into beta-readers and manuscript reviews in the next section.)

If you're reading this book, you probably don't intend to submit your manuscript to a publisher, but before sending it to an editor, imagine that you are.

If you think you'd be embarrassed to submit your current 'final draft' to a publisher, it's not a final draft yet and it still needs work. A final draft should be something you are proud of.

Sure, editors earn their salaries by enhancing manuscripts, yet it's unreasonable to expect them to transform fundamentally flawed material into a flawless masterpiece.

So, first steps after the initial brain-dump/getting-words-onto-paper? The re-read. Yes, it sounds dull, but it's so important.

After finally typing the last word in the last chapter of your manuscript (MS), you just want to get it out there for the world to see, but have patience. Your manuscript has probably taken you months to write, maybe even years; it's your baby! So, make the effort to go the extra mile and don't rush the final straight to the finish line.

Publishing is a game of endurance, not a sprint.

So re-read your manuscript; even read it out loud. It is amazing how much of a difference hearing your own MS can make. You may think your MS reads fluently until you read it out loud and are suddenly stumbling over the sentences wondering *how the hell did I ever think that made sense?*

2) *Beta-Readers/Manuscript Review*

After the initial re-read, you might have made some tweaks along the way or made notes about changes you need to make. Well done—this is your first round of edits complete! See, it wasn't that scary, was it?

Now? Re-read it again. Joking! (But not really.)

You don't *need* to re-read the whole manuscript again, but it's good practice to re-read the sections you changed to make sure they flow and remain in context with the rest of the MS, especially if you've swapped around the order of your chapters. Check you've maintained the language and tone that you want to instil throughout the MS.

Once you are happy with the way your first round of edits sound, it's time for someone else to read it.

This person will ideally be someone from your target audience so they can give you some real constructive feedback. In the book world, the term for the person reviewing your book is a 'beta-reader', or manuscript reviewer.

You can hire a professional beta-reader (if you're using a search engine, the term 'manuscript reviewer' will also give you similar results), but utilising the book community and people you know is a really good way for self-publishing authors to basically get a manuscript review done for free.

Facebook groups are an especially great place to pick up beta-readers as people are keen to help and learn, potentially in exchange for help with their own manuscript one day. But if you're opting for a freebie from someone you don't know, choose wisely.

The aim of the beta-reader is for them to offer constructive feedback that you can then take away, work with, and apply to the next round of edits. You'll collate their responses and make any changes as required.

Let's refer to the '*Early Stages of Marketing*' chapter in this book; being considerate about the beta-readers you choose can be a very tactical move. Think about the advice given in the marketing chapter: *it's mandatory to drum up excitement around your book prior to launch day*. If you pick someone who's not interested in non-fiction, let alone your niche, you're missing out on a crucial opportunity to use someone who would *really* get excited about reading your book.

For example, you wouldn't ask your dad to beta-read your hormone health book—he's probably the opposite of your target audience. Besides, you should avoid family for this task where necessary; generally speaking, family are already on board with promoting your book, so again, you don't need to waste this beta-reader position on a family member who's already sold. (Of course, if they genuinely just want to read it and offer advice, that's fine! Just remember that their opinions come from a place that don't necessarily match your ICA.)

There's no right or wrong answer to how many beta-readers you should enlist to read your MS. Just remember, these readers are going to be providing you feedback which you will have to go through. You'll then make edits based on their feedback. So, bear in mind the time constraints of enlisting more than three.

Here's what you're looking for when choosing your beta-readers:

- Interested in your chosen niche, industry, or subject
- Reads similar books to the one you're writing
- Potential future client (think ICA)
- Your peers/fellow coaches
- Someone who has written a similar book
- Present and active on social media
- Able to provide honest and constructive feedback in a concise way

If you've selected wisely, your beta-reader will be excited that they've played a part in the creation of your masterpiece, eager to read the finished copy, and thrilled to share and review your book at every opportunity when it launches—along with providing invaluable feedback on your final draft with the aim of making it even better than it already is.

This is the first step of pulling together your very own DIY marketing team!

Try not to take their feedback to heart; it's not personal, it's constructive. It's important for an author to have thick skin and know that criticism is for the greater good of their book. To make sure you get exactly what you want from your beta-readers, be specific about your requirements when sending over your manuscript. Here are some questions you might want to include in the body of your email to the beta-readers so that they are clear on the help you require:

- How clear is my message?
- How readable is the MS overall?
- What did you think of the language used?
- What are your thoughts on the order of the chapters?
- Are the step-by-step instructions explained well enough?
- What is missing from the MS that you would expect to be included?
- What could be cut from the MS?
- Do you feel like you would be able to achieve [*insert book's goal*] by the end of the book?

Your book should be going through an editing process after you've amalgamated the beta-readers responses, so it's worth mentioning to the readers to not waste their time nitpicking the more granular errors such as grammar and spelling and to focus on the MS as a whole.

Let them know how you want to receive their feedback. Make sure it's a way that is easy for you to decipher—make it simple for yourself. If you work well with Track Changes in Word, then specify this from your beta-readers. If you'd prefer to receive a separate document with a few detailed paragraphs of feedback, request that.

Remember, re-reading your manuscript and getting other people to read and critique it is going to save you money (on extensive rounds of professional editing) and embarrassment in the long run when real customers are reading your book. If you want positive reviews, you must earn them.

As an alternative, you could also hire a professional beta-reader or manuscript reviewer to provide you with a manuscript review and report. They will provide the same service as a hand-picked non-professional beta-reader, the difference being that this is their *job*. They'll be properly trained in delivering feedback, they'll know what they're looking for, and they'll create a thorough report with their findings professionally documented. They'll focus on things like the language used, the content, the structure, the overall message you're delivering.

Beta-reading might be their profession, but the same rules apply as they do for a freebie beta-reader: make sure the professional has a personal interest and is well-read in your niche.

The cost of hiring a professional beta-reader can vary between £50 to £500+.

3) *Hiring an Editor*

This is a very personal choice to make during the publishing process but a very necessary one. The number one aspect of book publishing that should *never* be skipped, is the editing phase.

Although, sadly, in the self-publishing world, editing is often seen as a luxury rather than a necessity.

Referring to '*The Self-Publishing Mindset*' section earlier in the book, you should now have an idea of what your budget is for publishing your book. You'll have seen on the Costs Table (page 17) that editing will make up a fair wedge of your budget. Trust me, the editor is worth every penny.

How would you feel if you were reading a book published by a traditional publishing house only to find mistakes, confusing messaging, language disconnect, continuity issues, and general dissonance all the way through it? Your first thought probably wouldn't be, *This clearly hasn't been edited.* Do you know what your first thought would be?

This book is crap.

Followed by, *I can't believe I wasted my money on this. Where can I leave my honest feedback and a two-star review?*

There would be a mark against the publishing house for allowing it to be published in this state. But when you are self-publishing, you are the author *and* the publishing house and it's your reputation on the line.

If you're an entrepreneur who aims to use their book to build their business, or as a sales business card, or to boost their credibility in their industry, or to get booked for speaker events, you *need* to produce a high-quality product.

Your book will represent you and your brand. A great book will earn trust from your readers and show them what standards they can expect from your business.

Here are some reasons why it's essential to have your manuscript edited before publication:

- Because your book deserves to be better (and can be better) than the final draft you've produced on your own
- Just because your manuscript makes sense to you, doesn't mean it reads well for others
- As a writer, especially if you are writing about your own experiences, it's easy to take for granted that the audience knows the context in which you are writing—because as a writer, you have the context! An editor will spot the context gaps where you've assumed the reader will know what you are talking about

- Editors have specific training in spotting mistakes, repetitions, discrepancies, structural difficulties, and generally improving your whole manuscript so the final product is engaging and tuned to your ideal reader
- An editor can take a manuscript from being disconnected and staccato to a beautifully sculpted piece of work that flows easily through the reader's mind
- They will take an objective viewpoint on your manuscript and point out sections that don't hold value and that could be cut (parts that you probably wouldn't have thought of cutting)
- Because it's important that the high standards in the book industry are upheld, especially with so many people self-publishing
- Because the world needs to be shown that self-publishing authors can produce great products to the same standard as traditionally published authors
- And basically, because you won't know how good your work can be until you've had it edited. You owe it to yourself!

So, once more for the people at the back:

Please, please don't skip the editing stage!

4) *Different Types of Editors*

The role of an editor is to improve and fine-tune the whole piece of work to produce a clear, polished, and professional MS. Which is what you want.

To complicate things slightly, there are three different types of editors that you should be familiar with before hiring one. That's right, there are different styles and aspects of editing, from broad content editing through to editing on a much more granular level. Some editors might offer all types of editing in one package, but most specialise in one type.

It's important to know which editor does what because every manuscript and every writer's writing capabilities are different. Therefore, each MS will likely require a different style of editing.

In this section, we'll look at the different types of editors and what exactly they do:

Developmental Editor

This type of editor focuses on the actual content and the book in its entirety. They are interested in improving the quality of the content overall. For example, in a non-fiction book, a developmental editor will look at whether the content is clear and whether the overall message is concisely delivered throughout.

If you have hired beta-readers, you may not feel like you need a developmental editor, as the content will have already been scrutinised. You will have already made a lot of developmental edits yourself from the feedback you received. However this is a judgement call you will need to make.

You may need further editing if you feel like your content and message isn't as strong as you would like it to be. Maybe you contradict yourself in places, or maybe you feel like the language you've used isn't hitting the spot with your ICA and the overall vibe could do with some honing.

A good way to decide whether hiring a developmental editor is necessary is to read other books within your own genre. If you think yours stacks up against the competition, great! If you think your MS could do with being pushed to the next level to compete, developmental editing could be a service to think about.

Line Editor

There are some grey areas between the job of a line editor and that of a copy editor and often the two jobs merge into one role. So, make sure you are clear on specifying the deliverables before handing any money over.

Traditionally, line editors focus on the stylistic side of your work: what kind of style you use throughout your text; whether you chose a suitable tone for your target audience; and whether you communicate your message effectively, but at a much more granular, line-by-line level than a developmental editor. Let's use this sentence as an example:

The dog jumped over the fancy fence, just in time to watch the feisty cat disappear, into the cat-flap.

A line editor would look at the language and readability of the sentence; they'd question whether 'fancy' was the right word to describe a fence and whether the cat should be disappearing 'through' the cat-flap, instead of 'into' it.

A copy editor would notice the unnecessary comma after the word 'disappear' and that 'cat flap' shouldn't be hyphenated.

Here are some other items a line editor would highlight in a MS:

- Overused expressions and redundant words
- Repetition of the same message using different words
- Unnecessary tangents

- Badly formed and confusing sentences
- Unclear instructions

Copy Editor

A copy editor will focus more on the sentence-by-sentence structural aspects of the MS, including grammar and punctuation. Their main job is to look for errors—not areas of improvement as per other types of editors. They will ensure that the sentences read well and make sense within the objective of the MS. They will also pick up on any spelling mistakes. If you're using multiple editors for different aspects of editing, this should be the final stage of editing to be performed.

Items a copy editor will highlight:

- Technical inconsistency
- Correct capitalisation
- Syntax and correct sentence structure
- Grammar, punctuation, and spelling
- Some copy editors also carry out fact-checking, especially for non-fiction manuscripts

Style Guides

Most editors will work to a specific style guide, which is a set of standardised writing practices that determine the way a piece of work will be edited. This helps to provide consistency throughout the MS and a guide that all the professionals working on your MS can follow.

There are slightly different style guides for different areas of writing. For example, fiction guides will differ to non-fiction guides, and a historical non-fiction style guide will differ from a self-help style guide or autobiography. One style guide may apply capitalisation, formatting, or punctuation differently to another guide.

An editor may ask you if there are any preferences you would like them to follow, which will help them to develop a specific style guide for your MS. If you don't provide preferences for a style guide, that's fine, the editor will use their own. So, make sure it's a style that you like! Ask the right questions and they will tell you what set of writing practices they generally follow. If nothing else, specifying UK or US English may be a good place to start.

Final Points on Editing

Editors will either charge per thousand words, per word, or per hours worked, so the longer your MS, the more the editing will cost. Remember, you do *not* need to hire all three editors! Only you can be the judge of which type of editing your MS might need, but here are some things to remember before starting the process of choosing and hiring an editor:

- Remember, an editor does not write the book for you! If you're struggling with the writing process, think about hiring a writing coach, joining a writing group or taking some writing courses. And if you want someone to write the book for you, you need a ghostwriter.
- Make sure you've completed one or two rounds of your own editing and ideally had the book looked over by at least one other person for feedback. This will save you money in the long run—if you submit your manuscript to the editor too early and it's still considered 'first draft' stage, the editor will likely need a whole extra round of editing just to pick up the things you should have spotted yourself. (And if they accept your manuscript in this state, the extra editing will cost you more money!)
- Even if you *are* an editor, it is not recommended to edit your own work. It's not about your editing skills; it's about what you miss being the only pair of eyes working on your MS.
- Once you receive your MS back from the editor, you'll need to go through and accept/reject any changes they have made. It's a good idea to perform a final read-through of the whole MS before you officially sign off on your edited final draft and progress onto the proofreading stage.

5) *Proofreading*

Proofreading is the final stage of editing your book will go through before it is ready to be uploaded to any self-publishing platform. A proofreader goes over your MS with a fine-tooth comb to spot any additional mistakes that you or the editor may have missed.

A proofreader will focus on punctuation, spelling mistakes, font use, font size, contents page accuracy, double spacing and the other much more granular aspects of an MS. A proofreader is the final gatekeeper your MS must impress and pass through before being accepted for publishing.

There is debate as to whether formatting comes before or after the final proofread.

As a publishing company, we have tried both systems, and we prefer to use the protocol of completing the proofreading before the formatting. The reason being that if any changes are made by the proofreader after the formatting (there will be), the MS will need to be sent back to the formatter to be reformatted. This will cost extra if outsourcing the formatting, or just be very annoying if you're doing it yourself.

The argument for proofreading after formatting is also a valid one, with the idea that proofreading spots any formatting mistakes like whether the pages have been numbered correctly. It's kind of a chicken-and-egg situation!

However, there is an opportunity for the publisher and author to spot any mistakes missed by the proofreader during the final proofread of the physical proof copy.

The fact is that even once your book is published, you may find that a few minor errors have slipped through the net, and if you do notice any, it might be tempting to just pretend you haven't seen them—ignorance is not always bliss and your readers will notice them if you don't make the amends!

Proofreading is one of the stages of self-publishing that you *could* get away with doing yourself. Being so familiar with your manuscript, you may not spot as many of the mistakes as a professional might, but it's certainly not impossible to proofread your own manuscript.

It's easy to get complacent when proofreading your own work and run the narrative of *'there're absolutely no errors in this section, I've re-read this part so many times*!', or unintentionally skim-read your entire MS and then BAM, a reader picks up on a typo on the first page (the first page curse is *real*).

With self-publishing, it is possible to make changes to your manuscript post-publication relatively easily. But, beware—some POD platforms charge for these changes. (More detail about this in the POD Platform Overview on page 169).

This is the mentality you should adopt when proofreading your work: that any post-publication changes you need to make will cost you money. This will force you to be way more attentive when checking your work, because errors mean charges.

So, if you are going to proofread your own work, be super vigilant and have your attention-to-detail goggles on.

Here is what you should look out for when proofreading your own work (*Ref 2*):

- **Typos/spelling mistakes**—annoyingly, Word doesn't always pick up on all the mistakes, especially when the error is an actual word (for example, 'form', 'from'). There is often a final spell check performed on various POD platforms on MS upload. You can also run your MS through an online program called Grammarly.
- **Grammar mistakes** (your, you're, their, there, they're, its, it's)
- **Misuse of punctuation** (incorrect use of semicolons, commas instead of a full stops)

- **Consistent use of verb tenses** (although the editor might have addressed this)
- **Correct referencing** (complete information used, weblinks are useable and reference numbering throughout the MS aligns with the reference numbers at the back of the MS)
- Check for correct **page numbering** and check the **headers and footers** for consistency and typos
- **Correct capitalisation** (e.g., names and proper nouns: Dad and dad, Captain and captain)

If you're not confident in your ability to spot errors in your work, or maybe you just don't have time, it's not unreasonable to ask a friend or family member to proofread your work for you before you look into forking out on a pro.

As with choosing beta-readers, be picky. Choose a friend who's known for being a stickler with grammar or a family member who always has their head buried in a book. Don't ask someone who has never picked up a book in their life and whose idea of reading is scrolling through Instagram comments.

Proofreader Costs

Proofreading is the most affordable of all the editing services. Again, it completely depends on the experience of the proofreader, but you can find the costs ranging anything from £2 per 1000 words up to around £15 per 1000 words.

On average, for a 70,000-word manuscript, you are looking at around £400 to £700 for your MS to be proofread. It is possible to find proofreaders who charge a lot less than this, whose fees come in at around the £150 rate. There's no problem with using a proofreader who charges less, as long as they are good at their job. If you do use a less expensive proofreader, make sure they come recommended or ask to see some of their published work to ensure you receive a quality service.

Pro-Tip: *When hiring a proofreader, ensure they know exactly what you want them to check for in your MS. This is particularly important if you have hired a line editor or copyeditor as they will have followed specific style guides. For example, a copyeditor may have gone through and replaced certain commas with semi-colons, only for a proofreader with different writing practices to change them all back again.*

Where you can, ask the editor to send you some notes about the style guide they used when editing your MS. This way, you can pass the notes on to the proofreader and everyone can sing from the same hymn sheet.

6) *Extra Copy*

This refers to the extra pages in a book that aren't part of the main content, also known as the 'front matter' and 'back matter'.

Examples of extra copy include:

- Copyright page
- Dedications
- About the Author /Author's Note
- Foreword
- Introduction
- Acknowledgements
- Thank you for reading
- Contact page/How to work with me/About the Author

The layout and order of the above will be addressed in the next chapter, *'Formatting'*, starting on page 141, and the content of each section will be addressed below.

Pro-Tip: *Make sure you get the extra copy written before you send your work to an editor. This way they can edit the extra copy too—get your money's worth wherever you can!*

FRONT MATTER
Copyright Page

There is often a lot of fear around the copyright page from new authors who aren't sure what this means.

The word 'copyright' sounds legalistic and daunting, but this is a simple page to put together so don't panic.

The copyright page basically ensures that the content of the book is legally protected and that you have exclusive rights to reproduce, distribute, and display your work. It also makes readers, retailers, and distributors aware of exactly who owns what.

On top of this, if you ever get approached by someone who wants to adapt your book into a screenplay, the copyright indicates who the person would need to gain permission from.

If anyone uses your work without your permission, you can use your copyright page to seek legal recourse *(Ref 3)*.

You can find plenty of copyright text examples on the internet that you can check out and reword. This is the Raven Crest Books' UK copy and you're welcome to use it:

*Copyright © 2024 **[Author's name]**.*
All rights reserved.

*The right of **[Author's name]** to be identified as the author of this work has been asserted by **him/her** in accordance with the Copyright, Designs and Patents Act 1988*

No part of this publication may be reproduced, stored in a retrieval system or transmitted in any form or by any means including photocopying, electronic, recording or otherwise, without the prior written permission of the rights holder, application for which must be made through the publisher.

*Printed in: **[Country]***

Paperback ISBN: 0000000000000
Hardback ISBN: 0000000000000

Other items that you might find included in the copyright text might be:

- Credit to the people who helped put your book together: editors, cover design artists, etc.
- If your book was being published by a publishing house, they would put their logo and information here
- Disclaimers
- Edition information
- Ordering information
- Artist names and song titles with permissions language (if song lyrics have been used in the book and permissions were secured)
- Sometimes author contact details are included here too

An extra note on Copyright for UK and US authors

Luckily, obtaining copyright in the UK is free and creating a copyright page for your book is all it takes to make things more official. Your work is automatically protected from the very first draft of your book.

But if you are an author from the UK and your book is being retailed in the US, you might want to think about applying for US copyright. It's not mandatory, but your UK copyright doesn't automatically extend to the US; the US keep a record of all copyrighted work, and you can apply for US copyright using the below link (*Ref 4*):

www.copyright.gov/registration/

If you're a US author, you are not automatically protected and must apply for US copyright. US authors do not need to apply for copyright to sell their books in the UK.

Dedications

This refers to the page that comes after the copyright text in a book and is usually a short note written to whomever you want to dedicate your book to.

Some people simply dedicate their book to a loved one:

For Thomas

Some might include a note too:

To Thomas, thank you for everything

Some dedicate it to a relevant cause, charity, or group of people:

To all those out there who have been deeply affected by grief, we stand together

Generally, dedications at the front of the book are kept short and sweet; the main page for thank-yous comes at the back of the book.

NOTE: *This guide indicates the 'normal' formula used in a book's layout but that does not mean you have to stick to it. This is the beauty of self-publishing: your book, your way. And of course, this page is not mandatory, so if you don't want to dedicate it to anyone, then don't!*

About the Author/Author's Note

The 'About the Author' page can be used as part of the front matter or back matter. If used at the front of the book, this page should be about the author (you) in relation to the book. Provide context to the book by explaining something about yourself. This might be something that enables the reader to relate to you, or to have sympathy for you, or be impressed by you—whatever it is, it should confirm to the reader that they have purchased the right book, that it's going to answer all their problems and they can't wait to get reading. Like a much more personal Introduction. For example:

I'm ____, a relationship coach from Somerset, and I wrote this book to ensure that others don't have to go through the same struggles I did. My journey started like ____ and now I'm ____.

Personal Anecdote

If you want results like this, you're in the right place, and I can't wait to share my story and my advice with you.

If the 'About the Author' section is at the back of the book, this is your opportunity to write a bit of a bio. In fiction books, authors tend to write a cute piece about where they live with their partner and dog and how they spend a Sunday afternoon. By all means, do this too, but the more important aspects to include as a business owner are:

- Your credentials
- Your qualifications

- Your contact details
- Your social media handles
- Any information about how your readers can work with you

If you're using your book to help reach more clients, this part is absolutely key!

Foreword

A foreword is effectively a big juicy recommendation page from an industry professional who raves about your work and fully endorses your book—a block of text written by someone who isn't the author *(Ref 11)*.

This person may have also given you a quote to use for the front cover of your book. It's only worth having a foreword if you can get hold of someone who is very well-known and respected in your industry to write one for you (see *'Editorial Review/Endorsement'* section on page 57). The name needs to be recognisable, otherwise you might as well ask your Aunty Mabel to write it for you, as an unrecognised foreword author will hold no weight when it comes to social proof.

You'll need to make contact with any relevant professionals for the foreword at the same time you put together your ARC team, PR and endorsement lists.

Introduction

This is slightly different from a foreword and the 'About the Author' page. Whilst the 'About the Author' note holds a personal tone; the Introduction relates to the main content of the book. It will highlight the book's context, key messages, and themes that run throughout and will be conveyed in a more informative manner.

Now that you know what each part of the front matter is normally used for, it's up to you to decide which you want to use. You don't want to overwhelm the reader with too much front matter (as a reader, we just want to skip to the nitty-gritty bits, right?) so choose wisely and think carefully about the content of each section. Each section in your book should add value and depth to the overall book; don't just include an introduction for the hell of it because you think you should.

BACK MATTER
Acknowledgements

This is your Oscar acceptance speech and your chance to thank everyone who has made your book possible. Again, this is *your* book, so you can literally thank anyone: your mum, your dad, other family members, your high school biology teacher, your local supermarket for the supply of writing biscuits. You get the picture.

On a serious note, the acknowledgement section is a great place to thank any freelancers or small businesses who have helped you along the way (Hi!). As a small business owner yourself, you know how important referrals are, and this is your chance to show your support and rave about your book contributors. This might be your editor, cover designer, formatter, or all the people who beta-read your book for you.

Maybe you used a course or training academy to get you to where you needed to be in your career.

Maybe you want to shout out to the amazing book that guided you seamlessly through your self-publishing journey (ahem). You know who your people are, so give them a shout!

Thank You for Reading

Exactly what it says on the tin, and this does not need to be an essay. It's a nice touch at the end of the book to thank the reader and to remind them how much it means to you that out of all the books in the world to choose from, they bought yours.

The most important part of this section is to remind them that if they loved the book, the best way to support an author for free is to leave an honest review on Amazon or Goodreads and to share it all over any social media platforms they have access to.

You can also encourage feedback from your readers via any of the contact methods detailed on your contact page. People often feel like they can't or aren't allowed to invade an author's privacy, so absolutely remind them that you would love for them to contact you and let you know what they found useful from your book.

Contact Page

If you've not already written an 'About the Author' or a 'How to Work with Me' section in your back matter including how people can get in touch, the least you should do is to add a brief Contact page so your readers know where to find you. Not as in hunt-you-down-and-stalk-you-at-your-home-address vibes, but just include your social media handles and a business email address they can contact you on.

7) *ISBNs*

ISBNs really have nothing to do with the editing phase of your book, however, now is as good a time as any to purchase them. It's a lot easier to get the ISBN stuff out of the way early on, so that if any of your freelancers need the details as part of the service they provide (e.g., the formatting), you can easily hand them over. It also means that when you're ready to upload your manuscript to the POD platforms, you can start straight away with the knowledge that the ISBN part of the process is already dealt with.

Let's start by explaining what the hell one of these is.

ISBN simply stands for Individual Standard Book Number and is a 10- or 13-digit number that is used to identify an individual book and its format. Each book format requires its own ISBN; however, an eBook doesn't *need* an ISBN.

An eBook is assigned a 10-digit ASIN (Amazon Standard Identification Number), which is used as their identifier online *(Ref 12)*.

Barcodes are slightly different. Whilst the ISBN identifies the whole book and can be found on the white label of the barcode, the barcode holds the information about the book—for example, the book's price. However, if you will only be selling your book online *(Ref 13)* you don't need to purchase a barcode.

If you want to purchase a barcode because you plan on getting your book offset printed (see page 212 for printing information) with the potential for getting your book stocked in retailers, you can purchase this at the same time you purchase your ISBN.

In the UK, the top ISBN provider is Nielsen, and in the US, the official ISBN agency is Bowker. You can buy a single ISBN for approximately £100 or a block of 10 for just under £200. Therefore, if you have any future books lined up, it's recommended to buy in bulk.

Once you have purchased your ISBN, that's it! You will need to display it on the copyright page of your book (see page 146), and there will be a section for you to input your ISBN on your chosen POD platform but other than that, you can now relax and tick 'ISBN purchase' off your list.

If you are using Amazon's KDP to publish your book, they can assign a free ISBN. However, this means that this particular ISBN will be exclusive to Amazon, so you won't be able to head to another POD platform and use it there too. Using a free Amazon ISBN also limits your distribution options.

To-Do List

- Order your ISBN
- Write your extra copy
- Re-read your manuscript
- Complete your own first (and maybe second) round of edits
- Send your MS to your beta-readers for feedback
- Apply beta-reader feedback to your MS
- Choose which type of editor you want to use
- Hire an editor
- Accept/reject Track Changes on the edited version
- Make any necessary final MS amendments
- Complete the proofreading process

Chapter 9
Transform Your Manuscript (Formatting)

1. Book Layout
2. Table of Contents
3. Fonts and Font Size
4. Page Sizing, Margins, and Alignment
5. Headers, Footers, and Page Numbering
6. General Structure

Formatting (or 'typesetting') is the cherry on the cake before you publish. It turns your final draft into a beautiful masterpiece. Formatting puts the manuscript into a readable format, in the uniform way that you would expect a professional book to look.

Formatting is a whole-book transformation, focusing on the following aspects:

- Layout and order
- Fonts
- Titles and subtitles
- Page numbering
- Headers and footers
- Page sizing
- Margins

- Contents page/Table of Contents (TOC), if required
- Consistent indentation
- Consistent style

The process of formatting requires good knowledge of how a book should look. You can be an amazing writer and not understand how to lay out your book professionally. Where do the indents go? Where to put a line break? What should I do with the margins?

Of course, you can hire a formatter to do this stage for you, which can cost anything between £50 to hundreds of pounds depending on who you hire. But formatting is a great aspect of self-publishing in which, with the right guidance, you can save money on hiring a professional.

If you are hiring a formatter, discuss with them upfront about their protocols for making MS amends after publication. Try to find someone who is flexible with future amends and that doesn't charge you an amendment fee for every change you want to make going forward. But don't take the mick! Hopefully, the proofreading process was successful and there won't be any further changes to make.

There are plenty of programs you can use to format your book (e.g., InDesign, Vellum, Scrivener, Atticus), but for the purpose of this book, we'll use Microsoft Word as our teaching example. This chapter will walk you through the formatting, bit by bit, so even the least proficient Word users will have a beautiful book interior by the end of the chapter.

Ready to give your book a makeover? Let's go.

NOTE: *Before you do anything in this section, it's advisable to format your document in two-page view. This way you'll be able to view your document like a book, rather than as a single page high school essay. You can do this by simply zooming in or out with the zoom tool on the bottom right. Or select 'View' from the tool bar options and select 'Multiple Pages'.*

1) Book Layout

There is no right or wrong answer for how you lay out your book, but people have a perception of how a book *should* be laid out and usually expect that formula to be followed. Humans like predictability, so if it ain't broke, don't fix it.

Unless your book's content is super different and outside the box, and turning the standard book format on its head simply adds to the topsy-turvy-ness of your book, it's recommended to stick with what works.

Here is a standard book arrangement including front and back matter that you can use to order your own book:

1) Title page
2) Copyright page
3) Dedication
4) Foreword/Author's Note/About the Author
5) Contents page
6) Introduction
7) Main content
8) Thank You for Reading
9) Acknowledgements
10) Contact Me/Work with Me/About the Author
11) References

For the parts that need specific formatting, there will be more detail about each to follow.

Title Page

This is the very first page you see when you open a book and this page is as it says on the tin: your book's title, followed by a subtitle if you have one, and the author's name:

Self-Publish
Your Book
Like A Pro

An entrepreneur's guide to
becoming a published author

By

Becky Warrak

Sometimes you'll find books with two title pages—the first one is called a half title page—which is a tradition that has been held onto from the 1800s. During this time period, the way the print process happened meant that once a book was printed, it would then be manually delivered to the bookbinding department. To protect the actual title page, an extra piece of paper was placed on top of the book. Eventually, the title and author's name was added to this blank page to help the bookbinders easily differentiate between projects. And then it just kind of stuck as a book publishing tradition!

So no, you do not have to create two title pages.

Main Content

It's good practice to start the first chapter on the right-hand page. This might require a blank page preceding it, depending on what content you have before it. You can continue this practice throughout the book if you like, with each chapter starting on the right-hand page. However, bear in mind that the more pages in your book, the higher the print costs.

It's also worth remembering this when thinking about the layout of your chapter pages too. It's not uncommon for books to be formatted with a few line-breaks before the chapter title, to create a space above it. This is purely aesthetic, but again, adds pages to the book. If you're looking to bulk out a book, it can be a good tactic to use.

2) Copyright page

There are generally two ways the copyright page looks in a book, which are detailed on the following two pages. You can use the copyright text provided in this book or create your own text. You may sometimes find the copyright copy at the bottom of the title page or on a standalone page. The choice is yours, but here are two examples of copyright page formatting:

Centre aligned

*Copyright © 2024 **[Author's name]**.*
All rights reserved.

*The right of **[Author's name]** to be identified as the author of this work has been asserted by **him/her** in accordance with the Copyright, Designs and Patents Act 1988*

No part of this publication may be reproduced, stored in a retrieval system or transmitted in any form or by any means including photocopying, electronic, recording or otherwise, without the prior written permission of the rights holder, application for which must be made through the publisher.

*Printed in: **[Country]***

Paperback ISBN: 00000000000000000
Hardback ISBN: 00000000000000000

Left aligned

Copyright © 2024 [Author's name].
All rights reserved.

The right of [Author's name] to be identified as the author of this work has been asserted by him/her in accordance with the Copyright, Designs and Patents Act 1988

No part of this publication may be reproduced, stored in a retrieval system or transmitted in any form or by any means including photocopying, electronic, recording or otherwise, without the prior written permission of the rights holder, application for which must be made through the publisher.

Printed in: [Country]

Paperback ISBN: 00000000000000000
Hardback ISBN: 00000000000000000

References

When writing non-fiction, referencing is so important to make sure you cover yourself legally. No one wants to write a best-selling book and then be done for plagiarism.

Not only this, but referencing your book correctly and using tangible sources to bolster your own knowledge adds credibility and authority to your non-fiction book.

Sometimes, despite your breadth of knowledge, you simply don't know it all. And that's OK, because there are other people out there whose knowledge can fill in the gaps that you're missing.

Here are some simple points to follow when referencing your book:

- Make sure your sources are credible (don't use Wikipedia)
- Reference someone when:
    - You have directly quoted someone
    - You are paraphrasing someone else's work
    - Using statistics that someone else has compiled
    - Stating that something is a fact when it is not common knowledge. (For example, "In England, many non-fiction authors

get in trouble for referencing incorrectly". This is phrased as a fact; however, it is not a fact. You would need to follow up this sentence with a citation of where you found this information. Such as, "As found in a study of 100 authors, 78 of them were fined for plagiarising in 2021 (*Ref A. Smith, 2021*)).*

(Ref 6)

Disclaimer: completely made up.

What to include in your reference details:

- Author's initial and last name
- Date of publication
- Title of article or book
- Publisher
- Subsection/chapter
- Page number
- Web link if applicable

Create a reference page at the back of your book and every time you reference someone else's work, make sure you put the reference details in the reference section, with a ref. number to link it back to the actual text in your manuscript.

You can also directly quote people in your manuscript like this:

> *'To be, or not to be, that is the question'.*
> Hamlet, Shakespeare

But you'd still reference it in the back of your book too.

3) *Table of Contents*

The contents table at the front of a book shows the reader exactly what they can expect to find in each chapter and how to navigate their way to it.

Without teaching you how to suck eggs, a table of contents should look something like the one at the front of this book. It might contain subsections if there are different aspects being covered under the umbrella of one chapter.

E.g.:

1) Formatting
    a) Book Layout
    b) Copyright Page

If you're writing a memoir, the contents table will likely be much more straightforward and simply detail each chapter, one by one.

E.g.:

1) It All Started Here
2) Realisation
3) Rock Bottom

Using bullet numbering in your contents page is a preference. The bullet number actually relates to very little, unless you intend to refer back to the bullet number later on in your book.

E.g.:
As referred to in Chapter 1, section a)

But if you intend to use your contents page as a navigational tool, you'll need to include page numbering as part of your contents table. You will usually find page numbers aligned to the right of the page, but the decision on contents page aesthetics is up to you.

E.g.:

1) Formatting..................................Page 22

You can create a contents page manually, or you can utilise a tool on word called a Table of Contents (TOC), which you'll find under the 'References' tab.

If you're a member of *The Self-Publishing Membership*, you can access a step-by-step video on how to create an embedded TOC that updates itself, in the 'Formatting' module.

The benefit of creating a TOC that can update itself is that after making any changes to your MS, you simply click the *update* button and it changes the page numbers automatically so they are correctly referenceable.

IMPORTANT: *If you're manually creating a contents page, please remember to update the actual page numbers on the contents page so they correlate to the correct pages in your book before you hit publish!*

4) Fonts and Font Size

Font choice in your book's interior is just as important as it is on the front cover—it's important that your book is easy for the reader to digest, and it's important for your book to look good. You may have never given more than two seconds' thought to the font you use (other than you probably have a favourite), but believe it or not, there's science involved with font selection. Choosing the correct font for your book is an important part of remaining "on brand" and in keeping with the message you are delivering in your book. (*Ref 5*)

With this in mind, there are two types of font: serif and sans serif.

'Serif' refers to the little feet you find at the ends of the lines that form each letter (like the font used in this book). An example of a serif font would be Times New Roman. Can you spot the only sans serif font from the examples below? ('Sans' means 'without'.)

Centaur
High Tower Text
Garamond
Arial
Palatino Linotype
Times New Roman

Of course, it's Arial: the only font above without the 'feet'. The above fonts are also fonts recommended by KDP as being legible, so if you want to play it safe, choose one of these.

How does the science affect the type of font you choose for your book? The 'feet' in serif fonts help the reader's mind move fluidly from letter to letter, word to word, making the text easier to read. Reading a paragraph of text using sans serif font is thought to be more taxing on the brain.

On the flip side, sans serif fonts are aesthetically pleasing with their neat, solid lines, and are usually used in titles and headers. If we're talking about the feel and message of the book, you might say that sans serif fonts give off cleaner, colder vibes. Whilst the slightly more elaborate fashion of serif fonts may be used in a warm, welcoming way, to invite the reader into the book. Is your book about strong hard facts? Or is it emotive, raw, and personal?

It does all come down to personal preference, but please, spend ten minutes thinking about font choice before you close your eyes and pick at random.

And don't use Comic Sans…

Font size

Your main content should ideally be 11 or 12. Anything smaller becomes harder to read and limits your audience. Anything larger is unnecessary.

You can be tactical with your font size choice. If your manuscript is a little on the short side, go for size 12 to add more pages to your book. And if your book is on the large side (over 300 pages) and your print costs are threatening to eat into your profits, use size 11.

Chapter titles and front inside title pages tend to be around the size 14 mark. Although it's not uncommon for title page font to be bigger.

Headers and footers are usually size 10.

5) *Page Sizing, Margins, and Alignment*

NOTE: *If you're following the course content as part of* The Self-Publishing Membership, *check out the video in the 'Formatting' module to see step-by-step how to size your pages, adjust your margins, and set the alignment.*

Page Sizing

You've probably not given much thought to the size of your book. A book is just... book-sized, right?

Wrong! Your book can be any size you want. Within reason. POD platforms will have certain sizes they can accommodate, and we find the most popular sizing for paperback books tends to be 5 x 8 inches or 6 x 9 inches. Have a look at the books on your shelf with a ruler and check out which size you like the look of for your own book.

Or, you can follow the crowd with the aforementioned suggestions.

Selecting the appropriate book size on your POD platform is one thing, but people often forget to amend the page size of the actual manuscript to match. If the page sizing doesn't match the book size selected on your POD platform, the approval phase will throw up all kinds of errors and your manuscript won't be accepted.

Once you've decided what size your book will be, make sure you follow these instructions to amend your page sizing in Microsoft Word:

- Layout > Size > Drop-down menu > Scroll down to 'More Paper Sizes'
- Enter your custom sizes in 'Width' and 'Height'. Check the measurement unit, as Word often uses centimetres. For 5 x 8 inches, the centimetre conversion is:

Width: 12.7 cm
Height: 20.32 cm

- For 6 x 9 inches, the centimetre conversion is:

Width: 15.24 cm
Height: 22.86 cm

Margins and Alignment

Using the correct margins and alignment are important aspects that will make your book look like a book. This is where you'll start to see the transformation of your plain document into a beautifully structured book.

Margins are important to get right to ensure that your text doesn't fall too close to the spine when your book is printed. There should be more space left on alternate sides of your margins to avoid this.

With your document in two-page view, follow these step-by-step instructions to correct the margins for book format:

- Layouts > Margins > Custom Margins to edit
- These are the margin dimensions we use at Raven Crest Books to get that perfect book finish every time:

Top: 1.93 cm

Inside: 1.93 cm

Gutter: 0.36 cm

Bottom: 1.93 cm

Outside: 1.52 cm

- Orientation should be portrait
- Choosing 'Mirror Margins' is key to ensure you get the extra space next to the spine

When thinking about the alignment of your manuscript, we recommend using 'justify' alignment. You can set the alignment from your Word toolbar under Home > Paragraph section.

NOTE: *If you justify your whole document, you may want to go back through and 'unjustify' your bullet points—justified bullet points take up too much room and look clumsy. While you're at it, you could decrease the indent of your bullet points so your* *bullets are flush with the edge of the text. Another handy print cost-reduction trick!*

Also check for anything that you had intentionally centered.

6) *Headers and Footers*

This refers to the space at the top and the bottom of each page in your manuscript. Author and publishers often (but not always) choose to use the header to put details such as:

- Book title
- Chapter title
- Author name

This additional information isn't strictly necessary, but the header can be used as a handy navigating tool if the reader is flicking through to find a particular chapter or section. The info used in the header can also act as subliminal messaging (not in a weird way). If you fill one of the alternate page headers with your name, by the end of the book, the reader is probably going to remember who you are! This is especially relevant if you are using your book to get more clients—you want the reader to reach the end of the book and have that burning desire to contact you and work with you. Subtly repeating your name throughout the book can help with that.

You could go one step further and put your social media handle in alternative headers.

The footer is traditionally used to house the page numbers, again for simple book navigation. These can be aligned any way you like; right, left, centre. However, you'll usually find them centre-aligned or on the outside corner of that particular page.

Here's how you can amend the headers and footers:

- Access the headers and footers individually by double-clicking either at the top or bottom of the page
- You'll find the main text becomes greyed out, allowing you to focus on the header or footer
- Type whatever text you are using and align it to your preference
- Use size 10 font (as per font section)
- You can choose to capitalise the text, or keep it in 'sentence case'

The text you've input will now appear across every header in your document. If you want to use different text on alternate pages, you'll need to:

- Whilst still in the header section on your page, you should see the 'Header and Footer' tab next to the 'Help' option on your toolbar
- Put a tick in the box 'Different Odd and Even Pages'. This will delete your original text from every alternate page
- Click on the header without text, and input your other header text

If you want to add different wording in the header for each chapter of your book, there's a handy walk-through in *(Ref 14)* at the back of this book from Microsoft.

Page Numbering (Footers)

The process of using footers is similar to applying the headers. Double-click at the bottom of your page to make the footer useable and type whatever you want.

However, if you're using the footer for page numbering (which you probably are), follow these instructions:

- Double-click in the footer area
- The Header and Footer menu will appear in your toolbar
- You should see the option 'Page Number', third from the left. Click on it
- Drop-down menu > Bottom of Page > Choose which number format you'd like

You can also get there via this route from the toolbar:

- Insert > Page Number > Drop-down menu > Bottom of Page > Choose which number format you'd like

You might find that the page numbering is only on alternate pages. If this is the case, click on the other page without the page numbers and repeat the above.

Be sure to check the font and font size of the page numbers. Update as required. Your footer font doesn't *need* to match the main content's font—this is a personal choice, but make a conscious decision rather than forgetting to format the numbers.

7) General Structure

The last thing you will need to do with your manuscript is to make sure that the general structure flows in a way that a reader would expect from a book. This includes indentation.

Fiction books are usually indented at each new paragraph with no line break until a change in scene/timeframe, etc. However, indentation isn't generally used in non-fiction books. Check out a non-fiction book and how it compares to a fiction book. It's probably not something you would have noticed until now!

A non-fiction book will generally be structured much the same as this one. You'll see the paragraphs split by a line break and no indent. Having said this, it's important that you don't use unnecessary line breaks.

Non-fiction editor Sian Smith has this advice when working out how to split your paragraphs in a non-fiction book:

"Usually, paragraph splitting is intuitive but generally you would use a new paragraph if you're introducing a new idea. However, if that idea or concept is a long one, you'd need to break up the paragraph into 'sub-ideas'.

It's also a good idea to include a variety of paragraph and sentence lengths to make the manuscript an interesting read." (Ref 7)

If you're publishing an autobiography or memoir, these types of books are classified as non-fiction, however you can opt for fiction or non-fiction style of formatting.

An important aspect to watch out for in general formatting is double spacing. If you've completed the proofreading process or had someone do this for you, chances are they will have looked out for double spaces and corrected them already. However, there's no harm in checking this again during the formatting stage. Here's a quick shortcut you can use for removing double spacing:

- Ctrl+F to bring up the 'Find' tool
- Next to the magnifying glass, you'll see a tiny downward arrow. Click it
- Choose 'Replace'
- In 'Find What' hit the space bar twice
- In 'Replace With' hit the space bar once
- Hit 'Replace All'. This should replace any double spaces with single spaces
- You can also do the same thing for triple spaces if you think you've accidentally really gone to town with the space bar
- This is also a handy tool to use if you find you've misspelled a word that you know you've misspelled through the entire MS.

And finally, when structuring your book, it's important to add a section break at the end of each chapter, rather than just hitting enter multiple times. Not only does this neaten up your manuscript and help the reader realise when a section or chapter has moved on, but when KDP creates your eBook, it uses the section breaks to work out when to put text onto a brand new page. If you don't put section breaks in, you'll get to the end of a chapter and the next chapter will just start right underneath the last one.

Here's how to add a section break from the toolbar on Word:

- Layout > Breaks > Next Page

One last nugget of info to add on formatting includes a bit of a 'love it or hate it' tool from Word. It's this:

¶ The pilcrow

It is often called the 'paragraph mark' or the 'blind P' and is used to display hidden formatting. If you click it, your whole manuscript will look a bit messed up, but don't panic! If it's driving the perfectionist part of your brain crazy already, you may not want to use it. Click it again to remove the markings. You can find it under the 'Home' tab at the top of your Word doc in the 'Paragraph' section.

When selected, this tool highlights how the manuscript has been formatted. The pilcrow symbol indicates where you've hit 'enter'/'return'. You'll also see dots between words—these show where you've hit spacebar. The small arrow shapes represent where you've hit 'tab' and finally, you'll see a long row of double dots followed by a pilcrow to show where you've added a page break or section break.

This tool can be useful if there's something glitchy happening on your page and you can't work out why you can't type a word in a specific place. Often, if you've added and deleted graphs or tables in your document, this can throw Word into a frenzy, and using the pilcrow tool can show you where the problem might be hiding behind the scenes. It's also handy to find out whether you've hit page break or section break at the end of a chapter.

Pro-Tip: *I'll reiterate, every extra page of your manuscript costs you more money when it comes to publishing costs. I'm not saying write fewer words and risk having less impact, but look out for unnecessary spaces, line breaks, and punctuation whilst formatting, and delete them. KDP calculates book costs based on the number of pages, so fewer pages equals more royalties for you.*

Chapter 10
Print On Demand (POD): Platform Overview

1. KDP
2. Lightning Source
3. Ingram Spark

Most self-publishing authors will use a POD platform to publish their book. Printing on demand means that your book will be printed at point of sale via the platform's own print company. This means there is no need to fork out on a garage-full of printed books that you'll need to ship yourself, carrying the risk that you don't sell any. Print on demand costs nothing upfront; the platform will simply take a cut of your royalties.

> *'Print-on-demand (POD) is a business model where products, such as apparel, accessories, or home decor, are produced only when an order is received.'*
> ***Shopify***

As you can see, it's not just books that can be printed on demand—there are plenty of ways businesses make money by using this model. Bought a cheap T-shirt recently with a catchy slogan? It was probably created using print on demand.

So whether you love them, hate them, or are quite frankly scared sh*tless by the thought of them, unless you have a spare £2,000 sitting in your savings account to invest in an offset printing (a type of mass-production printing) company and an empty (waterproof) garage to store them in, you're going to have to get to know at least one publishing platform if you're going to self-publish your book. The question is, which one should you choose?

In this chapter, we will look into the intricacies of three professional POD platforms—Lightning Source, Ingram Spark, and Amazon KDP—and see how they match up against each other.

First, some Myth Busting:

Aren't Lightning Source and Ingram Spark the same company?

Yes. They are both part of Ingram Content Group, which offers digital and physical book distribution, print on demand, and digital learning services. Lightning Source and Ingram Spark are two different platforms offered to authors who want to use a (POD) service to publish their book.

What are the differences between Lightning Source and Ingram Spark?

I'll go into more detail for both in a bit, but essentially Ingram Spark is aimed more at self-publishing authors with a desire to publish a small number of books, whereas LS offers tools and capabilities more suited to independent publishers publishing multiple books annually. However, that doesn't mean that self-publishing authors can't or shouldn't use LS.

But let's start with KDP.

1) KDP

What are the benefits of Amazon KDP (Kindle Direct Publishing)?

As a part of the Amazon mega-machine, KDP has the ultimate advantage that it is linked directly to the largest online retailer in the world. (The other POD platforms are also linked, but I'll get to that later.)

KDP is easy to set up from your Amazon account and it is completely free; Amazon take their cut out of your royalties instead of charging an upfront fee.

From someone who uses KDP day in and day out, the immediate advantage of KDP over its competitors is its useability. Give yourself a day or two to find your way around the portal, and you'll find it's relatively easy to use. For anything that isn't quite as obvious to work out, there is a whole library of KDP user articles and FAQs to follow for step-by-step instructions.

Another benefit to using Amazon's own POD portal is that you get a large and personalised sales page with options to add your own marketing graphics and an author page that readers can follow.

There is also the option to use Amazon Ads to help bolster your book sales, along with different options of deals and discounts you can apply to your book. You can even put your book forward for Kindle Daily Deals, which can often gain huge sales traction if awarded one by the selection team. And Kindle Daily Deals are free to apply for!

Did you know that Amazon also lets other POD platforms use their marketplace? For example, you can find books that were published through Ingram Spark on Amazon. But if you're an Amazon user, you will also find that, post-publication, your book will be favoured by Amazon's algorithms over non-KDP booksellers.

One of the most useful features, which may be taken for granted if KDP is all you know, is that you can actually make changes to your manuscript, even after it's published, for free. Of course, when self-publishing, you should always ensure your manuscript is produced and finished to the highest standard before hitting the *publish* button. But, in the cases where minor errors are found, it is possible to make the amends and re-publish. Please don't let this encourage you to skip the proofreading stage before publishing your book!

Another option Amazon offers KDP users is Kindle Unlimited (KU). Your book can be enrolled into the KU scheme, which makes your book available to millions of additional customers who are signed up to the KU monthly subscription. From experience, KU is a very popular service, and our published books are sometimes even being read more via KU than via other purchased book formats. However, this does tie you to Amazon and prevents you from publishing your eBook with anyone else.

And finally, paperbacks and hardbacks will be eligible for Amazon Prime delivery service, which means your readers will have your book in their hands often within a day of purchase.

One aspect of KDP that has been improved upon immensely is their customer service. It used to be really hard to get hold of anyone to correct any glitches or errors that can often occur during set up. But now, there is an email option, a chat option, and even a 'request a call back' option. And in true Prime fashion, the callback is impressively fast!

NOTE: For UK users, the callback function is on US time zone, so you will need to wait until the evening to access this service.

Drawbacks of KDP
When it comes to royalties, Amazon takes 60% of your book sales after print costs have been deducted. This percentage might sound huge, but it's also comparable to other POD platforms. Unfortunately, it's just the price you have to pay, and being the leader of the online marketplace, Amazon can be safe in the knowledge that they probably won't lose any customers with these margins!
Another sticking point is Amazon's distribution. Upon set-up, there is an option to enrol in Amazon's Expanded Distribution, which basically means your book will be available for a multitude of libraries and bookstores to order online. But remember, this does not mean your book will be *stocked* in any bookstores. It simply means that a customer can walk

into their local retailer and ask the bookstore to order it for them on the store's online system.

The plot thickens—this does not include *every* retailer and there is no way of telling which, if any, has put in any orders. Amazon also doesn't divulge which retailers it has signed up to the scheme.

An issue you might come across if planning a book launch is that Amazon don't allow you to print unwatermarked author copies of the book until publication day. So if you were planning a book launch, unfortunately your books wouldn't be able to attend!

KDP Summary:
Advantages
- Free to use
- Free ISBNs available
- Reasonably priced proof copies
- User friendly
- Personalised sales page
- Good for Amazon's selling algorithms
- World's biggest marketplace
- Amazon Prime delivery
- Book applicable for Amazon deals
- Manuscript is editable even after publication
- Fast customer service

Disadvantages
- It's not entirely clear where Amazon's 'expanded distribution' actually goes to
- Amazon take a big cut (but then, so do the rest)
- No method of pre-ordering non-watermarked author copies of your finished product until after publication
- Errors during the upload process are common, and not always easy to solve

2) Lightning Source

What are the benefits of Lightning Source (LS)?
What Amazon lacks, LS has in bucketloads. There are two main reasons why you might opt for LS over or alongside Amazon: the customer service and the online store distribution.

When you upload your book to LS, it automatically feeds into the online stores for Barnes & Noble, Waterstones and, strangely enough, Amazon. This is a great way for UK authors to get their books into the hands of American customers, and vice versa for US authors. Your book will also be made available for online order by libraries and bookshops in the same way that Amazon offers. Although unlike Amazon, there is a list available which details the retailers signed up to the Ingram Content Group's distribution partners.

Signed retailers are as follows.

Europe:
- Adlibris
- Agapea
- Amazon.co.uk
- Aphrohead
- Blackwell
- Books Express
- Coutts Information Services Ltd
- Designarta Books
- Eden Interactive Ltd
- Foyles

- Gardners
- Trust Media Distribution (formerly STL)
- Mallory International
- Paperback Shop Ltd
- Superbookdeals
- The Book Community Ltd
- Waterstones
- Wrap Distribution

US and Canada:
- Retailers
- Libraries
- Schools
- E-commerce companies
- Amazon
- Barnes & Noble
- Independent bookstores
- Walmart.com
- Target.com
- Chapters/Indigo (Canada)

As with Amazon, there is also a personalised sales page with LS, but it is less extensive.

It's important to remember that Lightning Source is not a marketplace but a backend platform. Using Amazon as an example, KDP is the backend portal and Amazon is the marketplace. LS is the portal but there is no linked LS marketplace; the portal feeds through to other marketplaces as mentioned above (Amazon, B&N, etc.).

However, and this is a big bonus point for LS—especially for people who might struggle with the technical aspect of publishing—the Lightning Source customer service is excellent. They have separate customer service and sales teams so whatever your problem, there will be a specialist agent on hand to answer your queries. You are also allocated an account manager on sign-up who you will be able to contact directly via email. With the self-publishing process often being less than straightforward, having the supportive arm of LS's customer service team in the background is most helpful.

Finally, unlike Amazon, LS allow users to order unwatermarked copies of their books before publication date, which, if you're planning a book launch, you're going to need!

Drawbacks of Lightning Source
The most obvious drawback is the price. You pay £52 per title upload, with an additional charge of £27.50 if you want to make any changes after publication. When you consider that the margins you make will total approximately £2 per book, these costs probably seem steep.

Furthermore, if you want to see a proof copy of your book before publication (which, let's face it, you *WILL* want and need to) this will set you back another £26 to £35! This is one of the reasons why LS is aimed predominantly at publishers who will expect to sell a certain number of books per launch and receive a higher guaranteed ROI. Publishers can mostly be certain that they will make back these costs in sales, whereas if you're an individual who is aiming to get their book in the hands of friends and family members only, you might want to rethink your platform choice.

For those using their book as a marketing strategy to help build their business, your ROI aims will be much higher and more monetary, so LS might be worth considering.

This is why we would advise that before you consider incurring these kinds of costs during publication, it's important that you identify what your book goals are *before* publishing. (As highlighted back in the *Self-Publishing Costs* chapter).

Once you have thought about your book goals, this might help you decide whether a costly platform is going to be beneficial for you.

On top of these sign-up costs, the margins that LS take per book after print costs are comparable to Amazon's, although represented in a more convoluted way! But you can work out your potential earnings on the LS compensation calculator, which you can find on their website.

Something worth noting are the LS delivery times upon ordering. Delivery times on sales platforms that feed through from LS often state four to five weeks, which can be very off-putting for potential customers. Although we have been reassured in the past by the LS customer service that these timings are incorrect and that two to five days is more accurate, there's nothing that states this to the buyer upon purchase.

Lightning Source Summary
Advantages
- Very responsive and helpful customer service team
- Book made available on Barnes & Noble (US retailer), Waterstones, and Amazon online stores
- Distribution available in a greater range of countries due to a wider spread of international POD contracts
- Pre-orderable unwatermarked copies of your finished product before publication date

Disadvantages
- Paperback only
- Set-up costs
- Revision costs
- Additional charges, including expensive proof copies
- Around 60% per book sale goes to LS
- Not as user-friendly as KDP
- Longer delivery times

3) *Ingram Spark*

Benefits of Ingram Spark

As mentioned earlier, Ingram Spark (IS) is a very similar platform to LS and part of the same parent company: Ingram Content Group.

The main difference is that IS is a free platform that offers eBook, paperback, and hardback POD publishing and is aimed at individual authors with no particular goal in mind of how many books they want to sell.

Luckily, like LS, unwatermarked copies of your finished product are available to order before publication date, which is a great benefit.

Disadvantages of Ingram Spark

Unfortunately, there is not the same customer service set-up at IS as its sister platform LS. But the interface is a lot easier to use and has way fewer options than LS, so there is less chance you will actually require assistance when using the portal. LS has more tools and options available to the user for more of a publishing model set-up, which is maybe why additional help is considered necessary and the extensive customer service facility has been made available with LS and not with IS.

Publishing through IS allows your book to be fed through to the same distribution partners as LS, which is a great advantage over Amazon.

Title set up is free, but any revisions made after 60 days of initial set-up are chargeable at £25 per file. Slightly cheaper than LS, and this is why it is important to make sure your manuscript is in tiptop condition before publishing!

Author earnings work like this:

> *'You earn compensation for print books sold through our distribution network, based on the retail price minus the wholesale discount you offer, minus the print price of the book you choose to publish.'*
> ***Ingram Spark***

Again, this works out very comparably to the other POD platforms discussed in this chapter, and there is an earnings calculator that you can check out on their website, which is much the same as the LS calculator.

One more thing: be mindful that when ordering proof copies, they are slightly more costly than Amazon's proof copy service.

Ingram Spark Summary
Advantages
- Free to use
- Free ISBNs but only for US customers
- Offers all three book formats: eBook, paperback, and hardback
- Books made available on Amazon, Waterstones, and Barnes & Noble
- Pre-orderable unwatermarked copies of your finished product before publication date

Disadvantages of Ingram Spark
- Limited customer service
- No free ISBN option outside of the US
- Charges for amendments post-publication

Chapter 11
KDP Account Set-Up

1. Set-Up
2. Description, Categories, and Keywords
3. Content
4. Proof Copies
5. Pre-Order
6. Hit Publish
7. A+ Content
8. Printing and Author Copies
9. Amazon Author Page
10. KDP Select
11. Pricing and Royalties
12. Reports

As per the previous chapter, there are other POD platforms you can use to publish your book. But for the sake of this guide, we will focus on KDP set-up.

KDP stands for Kindle Direct Publishing. It is Amazon's very own self-publishing platform. KDP allows you to create, upload, and manage your books. They also offer publication in three different formats: eBook, paperback, and hardback. With their print-on-demand service, you can have your book ordered, printed, and shipped via Amazon without having to hold any stock.

1) Set-Up

To set up your KDP account, simply type KDP into your search engine, which will bring you two options: log in with your Amazon account or set up a brand-new account.

Once you've logged in or created an account, you will see the KDP dashboard, where you can view your *Bookshelf*, *Reports*, *Community* page, and *Marketing* options.

The *Bookshelf* tab is where you will create and view your book/s. Click the big yellow *Create* button on the righthand side of the page to create a new book. Select your format (eBook, paperback, or hardback) to get started. You can create one of each under the same book, and once you've created the first one, the second format you set up will pull through the basic information so you won't need to repeat yourself.

From here, you'll see the tabs *Details*, *Content*, and *Pricing*. Work through each tab from top to bottom following the simple hints to complete each part of book set-up. If you get stuck at any point, the *Help* button at the top right of the webpage will take you to a fully inclusive FAQ of exactly how to do everything you need to do on KDP.

Alternatively, you can join *The Self-Publishing Membership* for walk-through video tutorials demonstrating exactly how to upload your book and create your Amazon sales page on KDP.

There are a few key points that you'll get to during the set-up process that need elaborating on, and these aspects will be addressed in the next few sections.

2) Description, Categories, and Keywords

After working your way through the self-explanatory steps on the Details page (e.g., book title, author name, etc.), you'll come across these sections: Description, Categories, and Keywords. These are the integral parts of creating your customer-facing Amazon sales page; your opportunity to pitch your book's contents to the world and tell your audience why they should buy it. Not only that, using the category and keyword sections efficiently help make sure that your audience can actually find you.

Description

As mentioned, this is your sales pitch to the world. If you've already written a great, compelling back cover blurb, you can totally use it in this section. You might want to pad it out or give it a few tweaks here and there to make sure it resonates in the different context of a sales page, rather than a back cover.

Again, do some research on how the best-selling books in your genre market themselves in the description section. Note what font formatting they use, too (bold, italics, etc.). You'll often find a successful book description page layout looks something like this:

QUOTE/EDITORIAL REVIEW/AWARD
TITLE (Upper or sentence case)
Catchy headline to summarise the book or who it's for

Book description/copy of back cover blurb
Include pain points to draw the reader in

- Maybe some bullet points…
- To hammer home what the reader will gain by reading your book…
- And how this book will benefit them

Finish with another quote or review. If you don't have any editorial reviews from reputable persons of interest, you can include standard reviews down here.

So, utilise this section as best you can and remember you can always come back and amend this section as many times as you like during and post-publication. This means that even if you don't receive any reviews before publication, you can add them into the description section post-publication once the verified purchases start coming in.

Categories

Categories are the group of books you want your book to be assigned to on Amazon, and this is where best-sellers are made.

You can choose three categories on KDP for your book to be featured in, and this means that if someone goes to Amazon and manually searches through the categories (listed on the lefthand side of the webpage in the Books section), your book will appear here in whichever category your book has been assigned to.

There are many different subcategories you can choose from, where your book will be ranked against other books of the same genre. At least, that's the idea anyway. However, over the years, the category section has started to be used in a tactical way and this is how many people now achieve best-selling status—sometimes unethically.

For this guide, we are going to focus on the ethical way to use categories to ensure your book stands the best chance possible to secure best-selling status.

Let's use meditation guides as an example. Here are some examples of the subcategories available to someone who's written a meditation guide:

- Mind, Body, and Spirit
- Family & Lifestyle
- Self-Help
- Religion and Spirituality
- Mental and Spiritual Healing
- Emotions
- Meditation

- Spiritual Thoughts and Practice
- New Age

Some of these categories will be more popular than others. When choosing your three categories, you want to utilise a variety of categories to encompass relevance, as well as providing the potential for your book to become a best-seller in that subcategory.

If you head to the Book section of Amazon, you can have a flick through all the categories that are available. Have a look at some subcategories that are relevant to your genre and have a look at the best-selling books in that category. A good way to tell whether the category is a popular one is if a celebrity or well-known author has a book at the number one spot. If it's just the top spot that's taken by a celeb, there may be hope! But if category ranks one to five are all big names, it might be worth avoiding this category if a big goal of yours is to achieve best-selling status.

However, just because you don't recognise the author doesn't mean that category will be an easy one to crack. If you don't recognise the author at number one, click on their product page and have a look at the number of reviews their book has received. If they have hundreds or thousands of reviews after a relatively short time post-publication (one to three months), again, this book is popular! And this category might be a tricky one for your book to climb in.

What you're looking for when choosing your book's categories are subcategories where the top five books have relatively low number of reviews. Whilst the number of reviews a book has doesn't equate to the number of sales the book is making, it's a reasonably good way to gauge. Either that or the book isn't good enough to warrant a review from the reader, which is another way the Amazon algorithm ranks its books.

It can take quite a long time to trawl through each category to see where your book might do well. Another option is to use Publisher Rocket by Kindlepreneur, which is a piece of software you can find online which does the category research for you and tells you where your book stands the best chance of ranking.

How to keep your category selection morally ethical? Choose categories that a reader would genuinely expect to find your book in. Don't list your meditation self-help guide under Environment and Ecology, even if you think you'd shoot to best-seller status in that category. Not cool!

Once you have found the categories you want to use, note them down and head back to KDP set-up to select them. The next challenge will be to find these categories in the KDP system. There is no advice to offer here; it's purely a case of sit and search! Some of the categories are only applicable to certain format types (e.g., eBook and not paperback), so if you really can't find the category you're looking for, move on.

This is probably a good point to say that if your book doesn't rank as a best-seller, that does not mean that your book is not a great book, and it certainly does not mean that you have failed in your self-publishing journey! Having a sole achievement of "become a best-seller" set in your mind is dangerous, because it's something that you can never guarantee. Of course, there're things you can do to make this goal more achievable and it's certainly a nice bonus when it happens!

Achieving best-seller status is *really* the outcome of:

- Effective and consistent marketing
- Reaching your target audience
- A successful launch followed by a successful first month of abundant book sales and reviews

Keywords

Similarly to categories, finding and using successful keywords (or phrases) will help your ideal readers find your book. You get seven keywords to utilise. To choose accurate keywords, you need to get into the brain of your ICA. If your ICA was looking for a book just like yours, which words would they type into the Amazon search bar?

Sticking with the meditation theme, your keywords might look something like this:

- Books about peace
- Inner Peace
- Calm books
- Mindfulness
- Positive affirmations
- Peaceful mind
- Books about healing

Don't waste your keywords on a word that already appears in the title or subtitle of your book, as these words will already be considered and included by Amazon's search algorithm. So, if your book is called *A Mindful Meditation*, then don't use the words 'mindful' or 'meditation' as any of your seven keywords.

You can play around with and change your keywords at any time. You can even incorporate keyword market research as part of your marketing in groups by asking people: 'If you were searching for a meditation book on Amazon, which words would you use to find the perfect book?'

3) *Content*

If there is any part of the self-publishing process that will have you tearing your hair out, this page will probably be it.

It's a simple enough page, and if all the previous guidelines about cover design and formatting have been followed, it should simply be a case of choosing your file and uploading it. However, if there is anything wrong, KDP will error message you, *hard*.

There are plenty of error troubleshooting guides on Amazon's Help pages but if you really get stuck, you can always contact Amazon's customer service team. (Or you can contact RCB, and we can run a KDP troubleshooting power hour for you!)

Top tips for completing the content page smoothly:

- Make sure you have your ISBN at the ready (unless you are utilising Amazon's free ISBNs)
- Make sure your manuscript is in the correct file format. Paperback and hardback formats require a PDF upload. eBook format requires a Word document, KPF, MOBI, or EPUB file
- Make sure you choose a book size that matches your manuscript's page sizing and the book cover size (***Note:*** Sizing options are slightly different for hardback so you might need to save two differently sized versions of your book sleeve)

- Choose no-bleed (unless you have any images, backgrounds, or illustrations in your book that reach the edge of the page, then select bleed) (*Ref 19)*
- Download the KDP Cover Calculator: 'Content' tab > scroll down to 'Book Cover' section > in the text directly to the right of the words 'book cover' > click the words 'Cover Calculator'
- Hopefully, by this point in the book this an irrelevant point, but avoid Amazon's cover creator tool if you intend on selling any books
- If you have purchased a barcode which already appears on your cover sleeve, select 'Yes, my cover has a barcode'. Otherwise, Amazon will provide you with a barcode automatically

4) Proof Copies

Proof copies are the first version of your book you will see in physical form. Apart from receiving the proof copy of your book being the most exciting thing ever, proof copies are designed for the author to check out how the book will look when it is complete and to check the copy for any final errors or typos.

It isn't mandatory to order a proof copy of your book, however it is highly advisable. (And let's face it, you've been waiting to see your book in physical form since you started writing the damn thing!)

However many times you have had the book proofread, it's almost obligatory that you will find an error on the first page of your physical book. Secondly, and especially if you have never self-published before, it's important for you to see the aesthetic of your printed book and how the world of POD book printing works. On the KDP set-up, you have different print options for the cover (matte or glossy) and interior (white or cream paper), and you might hate how the first proof looks with cream paper and immediately change your selection to white.

Your manuscript and cover sleeve will go through quality checks on KDP before you are allowed to order a proof copy. However, despite quality checks being passed, you may still notice some minor discrepancies with your cover sizing: the spine graphics overlap the front cover slightly; the barcode covers up some of your back cover blurb; the title is off centre. Some of these errors aren't obvious on the KDP previewer so checking out your proof copy is really essential to make sure that the final version of your book your readers will purchase reflects the quality that you want to present.

You will be able to order your proof copy once the KDP quality checks have been passed by hitting the yellow *Order Proof Copies* button at the bottom of the page. You will be asked which country you would like your proof to be printed in; choose your own country, or, if it's not listed, choose the nearest country. Currently, Amazon don't have a printing set-up in the UK for hardback format, so when ordering a hardback proof, you'll need to select one of the next closest countries (Germany or France).

Your KDP proof copy will arrive with 'Not for Resale' across the front of the book, but it's not intrusive enough that it gets in the way of assessing the quality of the cover sleeve. If you want to order proofs without this eyesore, other POD platforms do send proofs without this obstruction, which is particularly useful for pre-launch promo and marketing images.

If you are only planning on using KDP and were really hoping to take marketing photos of your proof copy, you may want to consider using a book cover mock-up tool online instead. The benefit of this is that you can create mock-ups as soon as your front cover is ready (a lot earlier than proof copies can be ordered) and the mock-up result is probably going to look way better than your attempt to use your mobile phone photography skills on your coffee table.

Once you've finished admiring your handiwork and have recovered from the fact that you've produced an actual book, remember to check the interior too. Here are some common errors to watch out for when proofreading your physical book:

- Chapter titles (formatting consistency)
- Contents page numbers (do they match the actual page numbers?)
- Page numbering (are they chronological, do they restart halfway through the book?)
- Header and footer formatting
- General text alignment (consistency throughout)
- Margin alignment (does the text sit centrally on the page)
- OBLIGATORY FIRST-PAGE TYPOS
- And typos/double spacing all the way through

5) *Pre-Order*

On various POD platforms, you have the option to make your book available for order before publication date. On KDP, you can only set up a pre-order for eBooks, but other platforms allow you to set a pre-order for other formats too.

There are reasons for and against setting up a pre-order. On Amazon, pre-orders work very well for well-known authors, celebrities, or debut authors with established, hungry audiences. People are much more likely to buy your book on pre-order if they already know who you are and are chomping at the bit to read your book.

However, if you are an unknown author with little to no marketing strategy behind you, a pre-order is about as useful as getting dressed up hoping to find the girl/guy of your dreams on a night out and then waiting for them to find you in a cave.

But that's not going to happen because you already have your business, you've read the early marketing chapter in this book, your audience knows who you are and why they need you, and your strategy is flying!

So, with this in mind, let's talk about running a pre-order. In the world of small businesses and entrepreneurs, a pre-order is an amazing marketing tool to use during book promo. Because even before launch day, whenever you talk about your book, you can link the pre-order page and people can order your book straight away. (And yes, you are going to be talking about your book *a lot.*)

On Amazon, as soon as your pre-order goes live, you will receive sales rankings in your chosen categories and in the overall Kindle eBook category. Whenever someone orders your book, this will work towards your ranking being boosted, therefore pre-orders can also help boost your sales ranking, but only if you make sales consistently. With pre-orders, if your book does well enough, it can also appear in the 'Hot New Releases' category on Amazon before your book is even published. (It can also still make this list without a pre-order too.)

If you launch a pre-order and you sell just one or two books, it's not the best news ever, but it's also not the end of the world. Best-seller status doesn't cling on to the success of a pre-order, but it does help with Amazon's internal rankings. As soon as your book becomes available on pre-order, the Amazon algorithms are working overtime to consider whether your book is worth giving page time to. So if you don't sell many copies in your pre-order period, Amazon might not favour you in terms of where your book is shown, where it ranks, etc. This is also applicable for the first few weeks of publication if you don't opt to use pre-order. The better your book sells in the first few weeks, the more your book will be favoured by Amazon's algorithms. There are other POD platforms where your pre-launch sales will actually count towards your publication week ranking, rather than be potentially detrimental, so if you don't run a pre-order on KDP, you might consider running one elsewhere. *(Ref 15)*

Remember, you still get paid for pre-order sales however many you sell! So, go into a pre-order launch with your marketing hat on:

- Pitch the pre-order at every opportunity
- Put the link everywhere
- Talk about it on your podcast
- Talk about it as a guest on someone else's podcast
- Update your bio links
- Add pre-order links to your website
- Use it as a lead magnet

There will be more ideas for marketing your book in the next marketing chapter. (Yes, marketing is so important for your book's success, there are *two* marketing chapters!)

You can choose how long you want your book to be available for on pre-order. You can set it for up to a year in advance (which is a little excessive, and if you're using your book to promote your business, is also a little pointless) or you might choose just to make it available on pre-order for a week.

It's not advisable to just take a stab at the pre-order duration. Think back to your publishing timeline: where does the pre-order fit into your marketing plan? What social media posts do you have in the wings to promote your book? What webinars do you have lined up where you can upsell your book? Do you think you can create a buzz about your book for a whole two or three months? Or will you have run out of steam after a week and be praying for publication day so you can relax?

Without throwing shade on the buzz of a pre-order, a negative aspect worth noting is that pre-orders can be annoying to consumers. In a world of convenience and Amazon Prime, people want things *now* and not later. So if someone has stumbled across your book (especially from a non-fiction point of view where the consumer is looking for a problem to be solved ASAP) but cannot buy it immediately, they may put off buying your book completely.

But let's summarise the reasons that you *should* make your book available on pre-order:

- It's a great talking point to help promote your book
- It can be ordered before publication date
- Use it as a lead magnet

- Pre-order sales can help boost your internal Amazon sales ranking
- Pre-orders are additional sales and additional royalties
- You could make the 'Hot New Release' list before your book is even published
- You can add A+ content (see page 209) to your page before your publication date
- Your Amazon sales page will be available before publication date, which you can direct clients to
- The publication date is set in stone (there are some grey areas around hitting *Publish* for eBooks on KDP which will be covered on page 206 in the 'Hit Publish' section).

Pre-Order Set-Up

The practical steps to set-up a pre-order on KDP are as follows:

- Head to the KDP *Bookshelf*, click your eBook and hit *Continue Set-up*
- Under the *Details* tab, scroll to the end of the page
- In the Pre-order section, select *Make my Kindle eBook Available for Pre-order*
- In the *Set Release Date* box, you need to type the publication date (NOT the pre-order date). This is the date that your book will go live after the pre-order period has ended

- KDP will generate a date by which you must submit your final eBook documents, to make sure Amazon has a chance to run quality checks before the book is published
- Once you have finished setting up the rest of your eBook and set the prices, head to the bottom of the *Pricing* tab. You'll see the yellow button *Submit for Pre-order*. You need to hit this button approximately 1–2 days before you want your book to be available on pre-order to allow for final Amazon checks. It's better to allow for the full 72 hours that Amazon set as their approval time guidelines, rather than hit *Submit* the day before and have your book miss its pre-order launch. Other platforms are more accurate than KDP when it comes to date setting

6) Hit Publish

As mentioned in the pre-order section, Amazon can be a bit vague with date setting when it comes to eBooks. If you've chosen not to make your book available for pre-order or are setting up another book format, you'll need to make sure you hit the yellow *Publish My Book* button up to 72 hours before your advertised launch date. This is to allow for Amazon's last-minute manuscript approval checks.

On the flip side, approval can sometimes take only a few hours, and if you've allowed for the full 72, your book might arrive to the show before everyone has even parked up at the theatre. In rare circumstances, technical errors can see manuscripts take even longer than 72 hours for approval.

However, you could use this to your advantage.

Knowing you will have to allow some time for your eBook's approvals, make the most of it. POD publishing is an online world. And the world only knows about your book's existence if you tell them about it. So, if they think your book is going to be available to purchase from the 15th of July, chances are they won't go looking for it before then. And if they do and they find your book live a day or two early? Lucky them.

A tactic you can use to make the most of these extra days before the 'real' publication is to invite your most loyal subscribers and followers to a secret pre-launch. Make them feel special and allow them early access to your book before the rest of the world. You can even use this as a lead magnet in the run up to launch day.

Another benefit of having this two- or three-day safety net is it gives Amazon a chance to get rid of any sales page teething problems. There can often be glitches that appear in the first couple of days that tend to sort themselves out (sometimes it's time for a customer service phone call) so this extra time allows for your product page to be ship-shape before your audience comes flocking.

Finally, you can only add A+ content (which is a marketing tool on KDP which allows you to add graphics to your sales page. We'll touch on this in the next section on page 209) to your sales page after publication, so an early secret launch gives you the opportunity to add this bonus marketing content to your page and get it approved before the big day.

Pro-Tip: *Please, please, whatever you do, do not leave it until your official launch date to hit* Publish. *Don't let your book miss its launch day!!*

The good news is that for print books you can schedule a release date from 5 to 90 days in advance which takes the guesswork out. Your book will be available at midnight on the day of your selected launch date. Amazon will work their approval process into this launch date, so you need to make sure that the correct documents are uploaded and your book is in a completed state five days before your set launch date.

To schedule a release date:

- Select your paperback or hardback book from the *Bookshelf* and head to the *Details* tab
- Scroll to the bottom of the page to the *Release Date* section
- Select *Schedule My Book's Release* and set your preferred launch date. If a date is greyed out, your date is too far in advance or is fewer than five days in the future

7) A+ Content

Go to a well-known author's book sales page on Amazon and scroll down to the section underneath the main book description labelled 'From the Publisher'. Here you will usually find some attractive branded graphics that the publisher has added to aid the book's appealability and credibility. This content may include mock-ups of the book, images of the author, quotes from the book, catchy headers, and brief information about the book.

The beauty about this section of the sales page is that because it's labelled 'from the publisher', if you can include some sales content in this section, your book automatically looks more reputable. And you don't even have to be an official publisher to add the content!

How to Set-Up A+ Content

- Make a note of your book's ASIN number, which you can find on your book's front page on the *Bookshelf* tab. You'll need this later on
- Head to KDP, and at the top of the page where the *Bookshelf* tab is, look right and click on the *Marketing* tab
- Scroll down to *A+ Content*. (Don't worry about the rest of the *Marketing* section for now, we'll get to that later)

- Choose a marketplace from the drop-down menu, then click *Manage A+ Content*
  - If you're planning on selling across international marketplaces, then make sure you also come back to this point and manage A+ content for the other marketplaces you want your graphics to appear on
- At the top right, click *Start creating A+ Content*
- Give your content a name in the *Content Name* box, scroll down, and click *Add Module*

Here you'll find all the information and dimensions you need to be able to create your graphics. Have a look around to decide which size and layout you want to use, make a note of the dimensions required or click on the layout option to find the dimensions, and head to your content design platform (e.g., Canva or wherever you usually create your social media graphics).

NOTE: If there is a design layout you like the look of but don't want the text included, just don't add the text when it comes to adding your images to the layout.

- Once you've added all the modules you want to add, click *Apply ASINs* in the top right corner
- Under *Add ASINs*, type your ASIN number into this box

- Select your book title/ASIN when it loads and click *Review and Submit* in the top right corner
- Apply the graphics to all your book's ASINs to make sure the graphics appear on each book's sales page

8) *Printing and Author Copies*

As we know, POD is an ideal solution for self-publishing authors due to the low level of investment required to have your books printed. But this doesn't mean that you can't also get your books printed the regular way.

Offset printing is the most common format used to print books and involves transferring an image onto a material. Digital printing is another format that can be utilised and involves computerised digital imaging. *(Ref 16)*

If you are interested in printing your own books in order to sell them on your own website or at an event, bear in mind that printing is expensive. Printing a low number of books (between 0 and 50) can often work out within the region of £20 per book. So you'd need to sell your book for at least £22 to make any kind of profit. And for this kind of margin, you're better off using a POD service and saving yourself the risk.

To start seeing a more reasonable return from getting your books printed, you really need to be ordering around 1,000 books. That's a lot of books. Consider that most self-published books sell around 250 copies in a lifetime. *(Ref 17)*

But that's not going to be you, is it?! Because you're reading this guide and you're going to market the sh*t out of your book and sell way more than 250 copies.

But think about it: 1,000 books might cost you approximately £5 pounds per book... well, you do the maths. If you are going to look into getting your book printed professionally, shop around, make sure the quality is good, and decide on a reasonable number of books that you can afford and that will bring you a reasonable return when sold. And that won't take up your whole garage if you don't sell them all...

If you do want books printed for the sole reason of having books available at events and speaker appearances, etc., there is another way! You can order author copies of your book from KDP, and the best thing about this is that you only have to pay the print and delivery costs. This works out to be a lot cheaper than buying through your own Amazon sales page.

Ordering Author Copies

Here's how you can order your author copies through KDP:

- Head to your bookshelf
- Find your published book, look to the right of the page for the three dots in line with your book
- Click the three dots to open a drop-down menu
- Choose *Order Author Copies*

The drawback of ordering author copies through KDP is that your book has to be published before you can make an order. So, if you want physical copies to be available for your book launch or event on the same day as your online book launch, this is not possible through KDP. Lightning Source and Ingram Spark offer a service where you can order author copies before publication day, so check out this option if you're using one of these platforms. (See page 243 for more information about Stocking Your Book Event).

If you're using KDP, opting for a secret pre-launch works well as an alternative way to order physical books. Ensure you order your copies a good three or four days before your 'real' launch date. However, check your book's delivery time; KDP does not operate on an Amazon Prime schedule!

Pro-Tip: *It is the legal obligation of every author to send one copy of their book to the British Library within one month of publication. That's right, your book will be in the actual library! Once the library has received the initial copy, they may request more copies. Or, if you select the* Expanded Distribution *tick-box on the pricing page on KDP, the library will be able to order it directly from a wholesaler.*

If you have only created an eBook without a print format version, this should be sent electronically to contact@bookisbn.org.uk. *Epub format is preferred, but PDF is also accepted.*

The address (up to date as of April 2024) is:

Legal Deposit Office
The British Library
Boston Spa
Wetherby
West Yorkshire
LS23 7BY

You might want to send a cover letter in your package to include the book's publication date, ISBN number, along with your name and address, to ensure you receive acknowledgement of receipt.

(Ref 25)

9) Amazon Author Page

Check out any Amazon book product page and, on the left, underneath the book's image, you will find the author profile; a small image of the author with a brief bio to the right.

It takes next to no effort to create your author page but completes your whole product shop window and creates a great little library to showcase any other books you have on offer all in one place.

The author bio is where the reader can learn more about you as a human. If they're on the fence about buying your book, maybe a relatable author bio will be what finally pushes them towards their credit card. You can keep this bio up to date, as you would with any of your other bios with details of qualifications, your career, and how people can work with you after reading your book.

Use it as an additional sales tool, another platform to sell your services from. But remember not to be a gross salesman.

Create your author page

- Head to the *Marketing* header on your main KDP dashboard

- Scroll down to *Author Central,* select your marketplace from the drop-down menu, and hit *Manage Author Page*

From here you can edit your profile, including your image and bio, add your books (after they have been published), view your book's rankings and customer reviews.

After you've created your author page on Author Central, hit *Go* under the *Author Page* box on the right to see how your page will appear on Amazon.

10) KDP Select

'KDP Select is a free 90-day program for Kindle eBook only. It gives you the opportunity to reach more readers through Amazon and Kindle promotions. When you enrol your Kindle eBook in KDP Select, it is automatically included in Kindle Unlimited (KU). Your Kindle eBook will also be eligible for Free Book Promotions and Kindle Countdown Deals (KCD).'

Amazon, KDP *(Ref 18)*

Couldn't have written it better! But let's dive a bit deeper into what's on offer in the above paragraph.

Let's start with Kindle Unlimited (KU). KU is a monthly subscription service that Amazon customers can use to receive access to an unlimited eBook library each month. Contrary to popular belief, Kindle Unlimited is not free within the Prime subscription package and stands alone as a separate subscription.

The benefits of having your book available to KU subscribers is that you are displaying your book to a whole new audience—an audience who wouldn't know your book existed if they only ever read from their Kindle Unlimited library.

'Free book promotions' relates to an offer whereby you can make your eBook available for free to customers for a limited time. This offer is only accessible for eBooks enrolled with KDP select. Amazon does not currently run a program that allows you to offer discounts on your hardback or paperback, however, if you want to run a manual promotion, you can simply reduce the retail price of your book on KDP.

Kindle Countdown Deals (KCD) are discounts that can be applied to a KDP select-enrolled eBook that extends for a limited amount of time. You will also see a countdown timer, representing how long the customer has left to secure this deal.

These deals are great because they appear in the offers and discounts section in the Kindle Store, which showcases your book and makes it more attractive to readers. These deals aren't available immediately, which means you can't use them as part of your launch strategy. However, these offers are a great marketing tool to use in line with some kind of giveaway you want to run within your business later down the line, or a great technique to boost sales after the initial wave of sales.

Enrol Your eBook

When you upload your MS to KDP, you will find an option to enrol your book into the KDP Select program at the top of the page under the *Pricing* header in your book's construction page or under the *Marketing* tab on your KDP dashboard (big yellow button at the top of the page).

The main requirement for the KDP Select program is that your eBook must be exclusive to the Kindle store for the duration of the enrolment period and therefore must not be for sale on any other platforms. So the only reason you might choose not to opt in to the KDP Select program is if you plan to sell your eBook on another platform.

11) Pricing and Royalties

One of the best things about publishing your own book is that you are entitled to the full 100% of your royalties (after the online platform takes its cut, of course). If you were being traditionally published, you may only see around 5 to 15% of your book's profits.

Amazon pay your royalties two months in arrears. For example, whatever your book earned you in July, you will be paid for at the end of September.

During the KDP set-up phase of your book, you will have found yourself on the *Pricing* page. When setting up your eBook, in the 'Pricing, royalty, and distribution' section, you will see two royalty payment options: 35% and 70%. This is the percentage of the book profits you will receive (Amazon get the rest). You might be thinking, why would I choose to receive only 35% of my book's royalties?!

Basically, the 35% is for public domain content which is content that isn't covered by any copyright or whose copyright has expired. You don't need to worry about this; your work will be your own and it will be copyrighted. However, you can use the 35% to your advantage, as part of your launch plan, and use this percentage to choose a retail price that's lower than £1.77, to tempt readers in.

For all other intents and purposes, select the 70% option, unless you just fancy throwing money at Jeff Bezos for fun.

When it comes to pricing your book, this is completely up to you. There is no right or wrong answer; however, much like book cover design, there tends to be working 'guidelines' that most publishers follow for specific formats and genres. You just need to do your research.

Jump back on Amazon's book section again and have a flick through books that are similar to yours. Write down the range of prices you find, and this will help you determine your own price; somewhere in the middle is a good place to start. Remember to check the different pricing structures for each format (eBook, paperback, and hardback).

You can also have a mess about with the pricing table on KDP. Put a figure into the top left box on the pricing table and watch the pricing outcomes change. The columns to the right indicate how much your book will cost to print, the percentage Amazon will take from your list price, and the amount of author royalties you will pocket.

An average amount for a self-publishing author to pocket is between £2 and £3 per book. Which might sound pitiful, but when you think that you haven't had to invest in stock and have had few overheads necessary to produce your book, it's not as bad as it first seems. eBooks often make the highest margin because there are no print costs. Think twice about publishing in hardback format because, in general, you'll have to price your book high to make any margin at all after the print costs, so people are less likely to buy it.

However, Amazon doesn't charge you any extra to produce your book as a hardback, so there's no harm in creating it. Even if all you do with it is order an author copy and have it sit proudly on your bedside table. The only extra costs you might want to consider when aiming to create a hardback book, are:

- Additional charges for extra format versions from the cover designer
- Additional charges for extra format versions from the formatter
- An extra ISBN purchase (unless you're using Amazon's free ISBNs)

When it comes to launch pricing, you may want to think about a special offer to entice people during that important first week of publication. As you'll have read, you can't use official KDP promotions for the first three months of publication, but you can amend the pricing from your KDP book set-up as much as you want.

KU Royalties

Royalties for KU work a little differently. After a customer starts to read your eBook via their KU subscription, you are paid per page read.

Amazon allocate a monthly sum each month which varies and is based on their revenue from KU subscriptions. They then add up the TOTAL page reads in all books read under the KU scheme and calculate the royalty per page read.

It's usually around £0.003 per page read. Amazon assign a total page count to each book when it is published. So, if you have a 500-KENP (Kindle Edition Normalized Page) book and someone reads all of it, you will get paid 500 x £0.003 = approximately £1.50.

12) Reports

The juicy bit—the pages that show you how many copies of your book have been ordered and how much money it's making you!

Hit the *Reports* tab, next to the *Bookshelf* tab on your main KDP dashboard.

This page is redundant until your book is published (unless you've set up a pre-order) so, after your launch date, load the reports page up and have a flick through the menus on the left.

Time for some famous last words: you can't break anything on this page so have a look around and mess with the filters. You can see how many orders you've made and filter by month, year, lifetime, etc. You can check the status of your pre-orders, number of KENP reads, and of course, check the total amount of royalties you are owed. You can even do some market research to see whereabouts in the world your book is selling most and which format is more popular.

Chapter 12
Marketing: The Launch and Beyond

1. The Press Release
2. Reviews, Social Media, and Mailing Lists
3. Giveaways and Collaborations
4. Book Signings and Launch Events

Although this second marketing section appears at the back of the book, it's important not to leave these marketing tools until last minute. Marketing is not a last-minute task! Read through these marketing ideas and then slot them into your publishing timeline however works best for you.

1) *The Press Release*

The best way to approach PR is with a positive but realistic mindset. Be hopeful, but don't expect to nail the killer primetime Piers Morgan interview on TV with your debut book.

A press release is basically a document that you put together that looks slightly more official than if you had just typed out a basic email, hit copy and paste, and sent it to everyone on your PR list.

It's a good idea to have some solid copy written for the email body, and then attach a PDF to really hammer home the details of your book and you, the author (aka the pretty version).

Here are the key items you must include in your press release:

Headline
Book-related statement or question to catch the media's attention. Think of this as your hook to get potential media to read your full press release.

Sub-headline
Single-sentence statement that covers who your book is written for and what value it brings to your ideal reader.

First Paragraph
The first paragraph will introduce your book and its theme (think elevator pitch), include who your ideal reader is, and why they'd enjoy your book. If you

asked a question in your headline, make sure you answer here in the first paragraph.

Second Paragraph
The second paragraph will expand on the benefits of reading your book. It can be bullet points describing lessons covered in the book (great for non-fiction), illustration styles (great for picture books), or even a character's relatability to present-day readers (great for fiction).

Third Paragraph
Restate the headline and why this book is a great read.

Final Impression
End with one of the following (listed in order of priority):
- Positive trade review
- Notable endorsement
- Portion of foreword
- Memorable pull-quote from book

About the Author
Your author bio in one to two paragraphs. Ideas to include:
- Credentials/notable achievements (related to your book's content)
- Awards received
- Qualifications and certifications
- Previous publications
- Writing style
- Preferred genre

- Themes/topics
- Personal interests
- Hobbies
- Hometown
- Homelife (spouses, kids, pets)
- Contact information
- Author website link
- Author email

About the Publisher (if relevant)
Paragraph about publisher including website link.

Book Details
- Full-colour photo of book cover
- Title
- Author name
- Illustrator name
- Publisher
- Publication date
- Price
- ISBN
- Page count
- Any special binding/packaging descriptions

(With special thanks to Erika Sargent, The Author Marketer for her expert contributions to this section, Ref 21)

Follow this template and you'll have an impressive book press release written in no time, ready to send out! There is also a visual template you can access in the 'PR' module of *The Self-Publishing Membership*.

You'll need to tailor the email body of your press release, too, depending on who it's being sent to. For example, a press release to a TV show will be worded slightly differently to a podcast guest request.

A good time to start contacting your list of editorial reviewers is roughly two to three months before your launch date. If you don't have that much time to play with, just do it as early as possible.

Remember, these are the big guns who are going to endorse your book and act as your ultimate social proof, and they're probably very busy, as are their agents. This is why your first contact with them needs to be as early as possible. You can use the same press release for editorial reviews that you created for media contact, just tweak your email body to ask for review quotes and endorsements rather than magazine article requests and TV appearances.

Please make sure you proofread your emails—if you're copy and pasting, don't send an email to Davina McCall's agent addressed to the name of whoever you previously emailed. This is the ultimate rookie mistake!

Once you've gathered your info and created a killer press release to send to your PR/editorial reviewer list, make it look as attractive as you can. (Canva is a great tool for this to create a great looking PDF.)

When should I send out my press release?

Ideally as soon as possible. Media outlets tend to book their guests/content way in advance of the actual airtime/article publication—sometimes up to six months in advance! You don't want to receive an email from a great contact stating that they love your book's concept but you missed the media platform's deadline by a month.

If you're using your book to build your business, you probably don't have six months to wait. But if you're on top of your business's marketing schedule and you can plan this far ahead, it may end up paying dividends.

Otherwise, try to get your press release out as soon as you can; ideally two to three months before your book's launch date. As mentioned before, you'll be in a position to send out your press release as soon as your front cover is ready, which is why the design phase needs to be started so early in the process.

Once your press release is sent out, it's still not over!

It'll be unlikely that you'll get a response from most people straight away. Schedule a follow-up email in a couple of weeks' time. And then another email two weeks to a month after that, depending on your time frame. If you still receive nothing back, you might want to call it quits. On the other hand, what've you got to lose? Just try not to annoy/spam/hound anyone!

ARC team

At the same time you're sending out your press release, you can also start thinking about sending emails to your ARC team that you created back on page 57. It's a good idea to keep them warm throughout the process to make sure that they're still available and keen to be on your team.

These are people who you should have already contacted and who, if you've communicated properly with them, will be expecting your email to say your MS is ready to be read.

They will be expecting to receive a complete digital version of your manuscript, or some of your team may have requested a physical copy. You can't send your manuscript to them until it's complete, but keep them sweet and in the loop until you can. Gather any info you need; if they want a physical copy, you will need their home addresses.

As soon as your manuscript is formatted and saved as a PDF, you can send the digital advanced copies out. For the readers who want physical copies, send them proof copies directly (see page 197). Don't leave it too late when sending out your ARCs. Remember the goal of your ARC team: they're your team of readers who are going to shout from the rooftops about your book and (hopefully) have an amazing (but honest) review waiting for you as soon as your book goes live. So, give them enough time to read the book before you launch it.

You can also ask your ARC team to let you know of any errors or typos they come across when reading. Your MS should be proofread by this point, but that doesn't mean that your MS will be error free. If you don't ask them to report back any mistakes they find, they might not naturally feel comfortable to do so, so make a point to mention it. Your ARC team are valuable extra eyes on your MS before its release.

You may also want to encourage your ARC readers to purchase a copy of your book to ensure that if they do leave a review on Amazon, it will be a verified purchase. How you do this is up to you! But a good way to entice them is to make your pre-order launch price (or initial eBook retail price) a bit cheaper than the price you would want your book to retail at. This price wouldn't be exclusive to the ARC team, but it does mean that making a purchase in order to leave a verified review is slightly more appealing.

2) *Reviews, Social Media, and Mailing Lists*

Reviews are gold dust to an author. Why? Two words: social proof.

In general, we are a society who like to do what other people are doing, because if enough people are doing that thing, it must be good, right?

When it comes to books, the more (good) reviews a book has, the more likely we are to buy it.

Take two similar non-fiction books; one book has four five-star reviews and one has 209 five-star reviews; which book are we going to deduce is the best and therefore the right choice for us to buy? We make that choice based on the belief system that lots of people with the same opinion know what they're talking about. This is completely regardless of the book's quality or how long the book with fewer reviews has been out for.

Editorial reviews take the social proof a level up, which is why they are so important—the goldest of gold dust.

Social media account popularity works in a similar way; you're much more likely to buy from a service provider with 25k followers than a smaller business account with 2k followers, despite the fact that the account with the larger following could even have bought their followers and the smaller account could be much better at what they do.

(***Note:*** Buying followers is not a conducive way to succeed in book marketing!)

The point is, social proof isn't fair, but it exists. So use it to your advantage where you can.

Book reviews are a great place to start. You'll already have your ARC team sorted and waiting in the wings to read the advanced copy or your manuscript and hopefully be able to land some editorial reviews. Next, you can choose to use paid sites such as NetGalley to boost your reviews.

NetGalley is a review site that provides mutual benefit for both publishers and readers. NetGalley is free for readers and very popular with book bloggers who want to read upcoming books before anyone else so they can provide current book recommendations to their followers.

'Publishers tend to approve requests from members who have a history of providing feedback for books they've accessed, and who can demonstrate their reach as an early influencer or reviewer. Members improve their chances of getting approved for more books by providing meaningful reviews.'
NetGalley *(Ref 20)*

Once a reader has left a review on NetGalley, it can then be shared on retail sites after the book's publication. Meaning that any reviews left on NetGalley will also appear on Amazon (and Barnes & Noble) if the reader follows the process to do so.
It's a pricey service, at around $550 dollars to make your book available to readers for six months, which is why it's a service mainly aimed at publishers. But it's there if you have the budget for it and is a useful service in order to get your book out there to relevant readers, to create a buzz around your book, and to generate reviews before your publication date.

Goodreads is another avenue, and a subsidiary of Amazon, where readers can create profiles, leave reviews, find book recommendations, make to-be-read lists, and see what their friends are reading. KDP eBooks are automatically added to Goodreads so you don't need to worry about adding your book, but you would need to create your author profile and claim your book.

The cheaper and simplest way to generate reviews is to keep asking for them. If you have followed the steps in the previous marketing chapter, you'll hopefully have created and grown a relevant social media following and started or added to your mailing list. Use these avenues to reach your readers and remind them that if they've read the book, the easiest and simplest way to help support you and your business is to leave a book review. Remember to leave links to all the places they can leave a review.

As mentioned in the Extra Copy section (page 128), using the back matter pages in your book is a good place to nudge your readers towards the review page while the book is still fresh in their minds.

Social Media and Mailing Lists

Having already started following the tips in chapter 4 about growing your social media accounts and creating mailing lists, this section is purely to remind you to keep going with your email and social media marketing.

Although to you, your book and your business is currently your whole world and you feel like you're boring people to death by promoting it, to other people you are approximately five seconds of their day on a social media post or email. And that's if they've even logged on that day or seen your post amongst the one million other posts they've scrolled past that day. Now that's not much time to make an impact in, is it?!

This is your reminder to:
- Be consistent
- Use visuals of your book
- Talk about the book's content
- Be excited
- Include pre-order/sales page links

And finally, follow up with your mailing lists and keep promoting your book on social media even after launch day. Your book's success doesn't reach its pinnacle on the day of publication—quite the opposite. If you want your book to be seen by as many people as possible, you will have to continue to drive its success.

3) *Giveaways and Collaborations*

This is a great way to raise awareness and increase the excitement and buzz around your book if things have gone a little flat. Or even if they haven't!

Think about what you want to give away and run a competition for it. Maybe you want to keep costs low and offer a signed copy of your book, but bear in mind, if you are an unknown author, this might not be tempting enough. If that's the case, you could collaborate with another author whose target audience is similar to yours, run a double giveaway and piggyback off each other's followers. Even better if the other author's audience is based in another country.

If this still isn't enough and you have the budget, throw something into the giveaway that your audience can't refuse like a £100 Amazon gift voucher.

Remember, the purpose of the giveaway is to gain exposure for your book, so write your copy accordingly so people will share and tag and get more people interested.

Another idea to boost book sales directly would be to run a competition such as, 'Buy my book within these dates and be entered into the prize draw to win a £100 Waterstones/Barnes & Noble voucher'. For people who were on the brink of purchasing your book, this might just be enough to tip them over the edge.

Get imaginative and work to your budget. But remember not to spend more than you expect to make on book sales or post–book launch business revenue!

Three months after your publication date, remember you can utilise your KDP Select enrolment (page 218) and run a free price promotion or Kindle Countdown offer to drive more sales.

4) *Book Signings and Launch Events*

When authors are traditionally published through a traditional publishing house, a book signing can often be included as part of the contract they sign, especially if they are a celebrity.

Just because you're self-publishing doesn't mean you have to miss out on this aspect of publishing! A book signing is what you make it, but be realistic—your book signing event may not look like people queueing round the corner of Waterstones or Barnes & Noble, waiting to catch a glimpse of this new up-and-coming non-fiction author. But that's OK!

Think about what a 'book signing' means to you. Is it you sitting with a pile of books at a neat table in your local bookshop, beaming from ear to ear with family and friends all around you and a few glasses of champers? And of course, a snap for the 'gram.

Is it more than the physical aspect and gimmick of signing books itself? Is it a chance for you to invite your most loyal followers and existing clients to come and meet you in person? Maybe at a local pub or restaurant or function room where you can sign books and network with each other.

Or is it about making the most of the opportunity to bring together your target audience? Do you want to provide your followers and clients, old and new, with a proper event? Something they can benefit from? Is this a perfect opportunity to host a talk where you pick a subject mentioned in your book and dive deeper into it? Can you turn the day into a 'Meet the Author of *[insert book title]* and Learn How to Solve This Problem in Just 10 Days', where not only will your audience probably leave having purchased a copy of your book but will have also met you in person, built a connection, and know exactly who they're going to turn to when they're ready to sign up for the coaching they require?

However you decide to manage your launch, be creative, and do what works for your business and your book. Think about where your target audience would want to hang out with you—if your ICA could think of a million different things they'd rather do on a Saturday morning than rock up to a bookstore, then hosting a signing there is probably the wrong thing to do. However, if your ICA loves a Saturday morning yoga class, work with it:

Join online coach and author [insert name] for a free morning of yoga, coffee, and book signings.

Don't just take yourself to the nearest bookstore with no planning and a load of books only to be left dejected if no one turns up. Even if a book signing feels like the expected thing for an author to do, a book signing is not a rite of passage. You are still an author even if you don't host a book signing!

Remember to market it well in advance and be thorough in your market research to make sure your event is definitely something your people will want to attend. Your book signing event doesn't even have to be on your launch day. This is the beauty of self-publishing: you can literally run things exactly how you like!

Stocking Your Book Event

If you've decided to host some kind of launch event, you're going to need some books. There are a few ways you can do this:

Purchase Amazon author copies
- **Advantages:**
  o inexpensive to produce and room to make a good ROI
- **Disadvantages:**
  o Can only be ordered after publication date and will take approximately 4–7 days to arrive
  o These books won't count as part of your overall book sales and therefore won't contribute to your sales ranking
  o They also won't count as a verified purchase so if anyone leaves a review after reading, it won't be Amazon verified

Print your own copies
- **Advantages:**
  o Can order these to be ready for your launch date
  o Likely better quality than Amazon's printing
- **Disadvantages:**
  o Expensive if only ordering a few
  o Think of storage and risk of no ROI if you're ordering a lot

- Won't count towards your Amazon sales rankings unless you sell your books

Buy your own book from Amazon
- **Advantages:**
- Prime delivery
- Purchases will count towards your sales ranking (this does not mean that you should buy 100 of your own books just to reach best-seller status!)
- **Disadvantages:**
- You pay the full retail price
- Reader reviews won't be verified
- You won't be able to order them until post-publication. However, you can 'hit publish' early on KDP and have a secret pre-launch to ensure you *can* order your books before the 'official' launch day

Use a QR code
- **Advantages:**
- Takes customer directly to Amazon sales page where they will complete the order
- Orders count towards your Amazon ranking
- Easy and cashless
- Reviews will appear as verified purchases on Amazon
- **Disadvantages:**
- No physical book at book signing and therefore no book to be signed

Order author copies from Lightning Source or Ingram Spark

- **Advantages:**
  - You can order author copies before your publication date meaning they will arrive on time for your launch
- **Disadvantages:**
  - They won't count towards any sales rankings
  - Reader reviews won't be verified

As far as the rest of your book marketing journey goes, now that you have the tools you need, it's up to you to use them as best you can. Remember, it's *your* self-publishing journey, so you can do as little or as much marketing as you like. But you reap what you sow: have your book's goals in mind throughout the marketing process and make the most of this opportunity to market the hell out of your business.

Remember, writing a book was a part of your business's bigger picture marketing plan. You wrote your book to build your business; reach more customers; improve your business's visibility and credibility; diversify your revenue streams; and increase your overall revenue. When you've finished publishing your book, take a step back and appreciate what you have done.

Have a look at what you originally wrote down as your book's goals. Did you achieve them or are you on your way to achieving them?

Writing a book is an amazing marketing tactic to execute, and you've just completed it! Be proud of yourself, and who knows? Now that you know the process and have seen the benefits, you might even want to write book number two…

A Final Note

Firstly, congratulations! I hope you made it through the book smoothly and unscathed and are now celebrating being a published author!

I hope you found this book useful, informative, and a bit less stuffy than your usual self-pub guide; I am fully aware that self-publishing is far from being a riveting subject matter! I have tried to make the content readable and engaging wherever possible, however there are limited ways in which to make an ISBN sound interesting…

My aim for this book was always to leave no stone unturned when it comes to self-publishing your book. I have read my fair share of "informative" guides and signed up to various courses and webinars in my time in my own businesses and am often left scratching my head thinking, *Did I actually learn how to do that thing I wanted to do?*

What this book might have taught you, other than exactly how to self-publish your book and market it, is that there is a lot involved in self-publishing. And whilst you are now aware of the process and what practically needs to be done, you may feel like you need support, accountability, or just someone to talk to who is going through the same crazy, overwhelming, book-publishing journey.

This is why we created *The Self-Publishing Membership*.

The monthly membership was created to support self-publishing authors throughout the process of publishing their book by providing peer support, accountability, video tutorials, Facebook group access, and live bi-monthly check-in sessions with industry experts and the Raven Crest Books owners. Scan the QR code below to head to *The Self-Publishing Membership* landing page for more information on joining.

If you've made it this far and are reading this note, I would imagine you have decided to take the bull by the horns and hurtle full pelt into the self-publishing world! However, if you do get stuck along the way with any aspect of the publishing process, we are here for you with individual services to take the stress out of certain stages (ahem, formatting...).

Scan the QR code below to check out the 'Build a Book' services we offer and to book.

Finally, I just want to say well done—the process of self-publishing is not for the faint hearted, and you can be proud of yourself for showing your dedication to your business and for showing the desire to help as many people as possible. The world needs people like you!

If you enjoyed this book, it would mean the world to me and *my* small business if you would leave a review on Amazon or whichever retailer you purchased it from. As you know by now, reviews mean a lot in the book world!

I love to support self-published authors, especially those who have self-published with the help of my book! Therefore, I'd love if you would tag us in any social media posts once your book is published or email me a link to the sales page. Where possible, I will endeavour to purchase and read as many as possible, and you can be sure I will leave you an honest review. You can find our social media links on our contact page at the back of this book.

One more final congratulations to you, and thank you again for reading my book. I appreciate every one of you.

Becky
Raven Crest Books

Contact Details

Becky Warrak
Owner of Raven Crest Books
Publisher and Self-Publishing Coach

Instagram: @Ravencrest_Books
Facebook: @RavenCrestBooksClub
Twitter/X: @Ravencrest_Books
Website: ravencrestbooks.co.uk /.com
Email: becky@ravencrestbooks.com

Becky lives with husband and business co-owner Omar and their three young boys. After leaving the UK in 2022 for beautiful Turkey, they are currently back residing in Northampton, UK… for now!

References

1. Statista, January 2024, *Most popular social networks worldwide as of January 2024, ranked by number of monthly active users*, www.statista.com/statistics/272014/global-social-networks-ranked-by-number-of-users/

2. Oxbridge Editing Blog, November 2019, *The ultimate proofreading checklist*, https://www.oxbridgeediting.co.uk/blog/the-ultimate-proofreading-checklist/

3. Paper True, January 2024, *How to copyright a book in 2024*, www.papertrue.com/blog/how-to-copyright-a-book/

4. Book Beaver, April 2021, *How to copyright a book* by Rebecca Munton, www.bookbeaver.co.uk/blog/how-to-copyright-a-book#one

5. Ingram Spark, May 2021, *The best fonts for books* by Michele DeFilippo, https://www.ingramspark.com/blog/best-fonts-for-books

6. Craft Your Content, January 2016, *A very brief guide to citing sources in a bibliography* by Ben Barber, www.craftyourcontent.com/citing-sources-bibliography/

7. Direct quote from Sian Smith, March 2024, Editor at Sian Smith Editorial, https://www.siansmitheditorial.co.uk/

8. Statista, February 2024, *Market share of leading business process management (graphics) software vendors worldwide in 2024, by product*, by Lionel Sujay Vailshery,

www.statista.com/statistics/1369176/worldwide-graphics-market-share/#:~:text=Adobe%20Photoshop%20leads%20the%20graphics,28%20and%2013%20percent%20respectively

9. Canva, *Free Media License Agreement*, www.canva.com/policies/free-media-license-agreement-2022-01-03/

10. G2, *Best stock photos websites* by Priya Patel, www.g2.com/categories/stock-photos

11. MasterClass, August 2021, *What's the difference? Preface, prologue, introduction and foreword*, www.masterclass.com/articles/preface-prologue-introduction-difference#IPxID6tsAHNtpL5MNEDeO

12. Ingram Spark, December 2020, *ISBNs: International standard book number facts for self-publishers*, www.ingramspark.com/blog/isbn-facts-for-self-publishers

13. Independent Publishing Network, *How to use your ISBN*, www.bookisbn.org.uk/how-to-use-your-isbn/#:~:text=Print%20the%20ISBN%20Barcode%20onto%20your%20Book&text=The%20image%20size%20should%20be,ISBN%20number%20below%20the%20bars

14. Microsoft Support, *Configure headers and footers for different sections of a document*, https://support.microsoft.com/en-us/office/configure-headers-and-footers-for-different-sections-of-a-document-94332643-a6e9-46aa-ab29-064f1d356db6

15. Books Forward, January 2023, *How do pre-orders affect release day sales* by Jackie Karneth, www.booksforward.com/how-do-pre-orders-affect-release-day-sales/

16. Sure Print and Design, *Book printing basics and what you need to know,* https://sureprintanddesign.ca/article/everything-you-need-to-know-about-book-printing/#:~:text=Offset%20printing%20is%20the%20most,time%20as%20they%20are%20ordered

17. WordsRated, January 2023, Self-published books and author's sales statistics 2023 by Nicholas Rizzo, https://wordsrated.com/self-published-book-sales-statistics/

18. KDP Help Topics, *KDP Select*, https://kdp.amazon.com/en_US/help/topic/G200798990

19. KDP Help Topics, *Set trim size, bleed and margins: When to choose bleed for your interior,* https://kdp.amazon.com/en_US/help/topic/GVBQ3CMEQW3W2VL6#:~:text=You%20should%20include%20bleed%20in,be%20set%20up%20with%20bleed

20. NetGalley, *How it works,* https://www.netgalley.com/tour

21. Information supplied by Erika Sargent, The Author Marketer, Instagram handle: @theauthormarketer, www.theauthormarketer.com

22. Search Engine Land, *What is SEO – search engine optimization?* https://searchengineland.com/guide/what-is-seo

23. Termly, *GDPR for dummies: What is the GDPR?* By Teodor Stanciu, https://termly.io/resources/articles/gdpr-for-dummies/#:~:text=The%20GDPR%20is%20an%20acronym,to%20process%20that%20data%20legally

24. Adobe, *Everything you need to know about hi res and high resolution images,* https://www.adobe.com/uk/creativecloud/photography/discover/high-resolution.html

25. Independent Publisher Network, *Author legal deposit obligations*, https://bookisbn.org.uk/legal-deposit/

www.ingramcontent.com/pod-product-compliance
Lightning Source LLC
Chambersburg PA
CBHW060149050426
42446CB00013B/2741